French Grammar

by
Christopher Kendris, Ph.D.

Formerly Assistant Professor
Department of French and Spanish
State University of New York at Albany

Diplômé, Faculté des Lettres, Université de Paris et Institut de Phonétique, Paris (en Sorbonne)

Certificat, Ecole Pédagogique de l'Alliance Française de Paris

BARRON'S EDUCATIONAL SERIES, INC.
New York • London • Toronto • Sydney

To the sweet memory of my mother
and to the memory of my father

All inquiries should be addressed to:
Barron's Educational Series, Inc.
250 Wireless Boulevard
Hauppauge, New York 11788

Library of Congress Catalog Card No. 89-17822
International Standard Book No. 0-8120-4292-1

Library of Congress Cataloging-in-Publication Data

Kendris, Christopher.
    French grammar / by Christopher Kendris.
        p.   cm.
    Adaptation of: Master the basics: French. c1987.
    ISBN 0-8120-4292-1
    1. French language—Textbooks for foreign speakers—English.
2. French language—Grammar—1950- I. Kendris, Christopher.
Master the basics. II. Title.
PC2129.E5K428   1990
448.2'421—dc20   89-17822
                                                                        CIP

PRINTED IN THE UNITED STATES OF AMERICA

012   550   98765432

Contents

Special Topics 131

Preface

This book is one of a new series of handy grammar reference guides. It is designed for students, businesspeople, and others who want to "brush up" their knowledge of French grammar for instant communication and comprehension.

Whether you are just beginning your study of French or have had some French and want to review, this book is for you. Previous knowledge has not been taken for granted in these pages; definitions and explanations are concise and clear, and examples use and reuse a core of basic vocabulary.

The complete grammar review consists of three parts: the Basics, the Parts of Speech, and Special Topics, all of which are outlined in the table of contents.

Occasionally I offer some mnemonic (memory) tips to help you remember certain aspects of French grammar and vocabulary. For example, if you cannot remember whether the French word for twenty **(vingt)** is spelled *ng* or *gn,* remember it this way:

Mnemonic tip	V I N G T
	T W E N T Y

Mnemonic devices are very useful in learning and remembering. Students learn and remember in different ways. What works for you may not work for someone else. You must think of ways to help yourself remember. If you think of a way that seems foolish, don't tell anyone; just let it work for you. One of my students in a Spanish class, for example, told me that she finally figured out a way to remember the meaning of the Spanish verb *buscar* / to look for. She said, "I'm looking for a bus or a car." How many mnemonic tips can you make up in French? Here are a few more: If someone asks you, "What are the five major Romance Languages?" are you going to say you don't know? Remember **FRIPS:**

Mnemonic tip	**F**rench
	Romanian
	Italian
	Portuguese
	Spanish

To remember that there are only four nasal vowels in French, hang on to this catchy phrase because each word contains one of the four nasal vowels:

Mnemonic tip	*un bon vin blanc* / a good white wine

If you keep pronouncing *un œuf* / an egg incorrectly, say this out loud:

Mnemonic tip	Do you want one egg? Two eggs?
	One egg is enough!
	One egg is *un œuf*!

The sound of the English word "enough" is very close to the sound of the French word *un œuf*.

There are many more mnemonic tips throughout this book. If I have omitted anything you think is important, if you spot any misprints, or if you have any suggestions for the improvement of the next edition, please write to me, care of the publisher.

Christopher Kendris
B.S., M.S., M.A., Ph.D.

How to Use This Book

In the chapters that follow, a numerical decimal system has been used with the symbol § in front of it. This was done so that you may find quickly and easily the reference to a particular point in basic French grammar when you use the index. For example, if you look up the entry "adjectives" in the index, you will find the reference given as §5. Sometimes additional § reference numbers are given when the entry you consult is mentioned in other areas in the chapter §. The index also includes some key French words, for example, avoir and être, with § references also given to them.

The Basics

§1.

Guide to Pronouncing French Sounds

English words given here contain sounds that only approximate French sounds.

PURE VOWEL SOUNDS

Pronounced as in the

French word	English word
la	yacht
pas	father
été	ate
ère	egg
ici	see
hôtel	over
donne	bun
ou	too
leur	urgent
deux	pudding
tu	cute
le	ago

NASAL VOWEL SOUNDS

French word	English word
un	unguent
bon	song
vin	sang
blanc	throng

SEMICONSONANT SOUNDS

French word	English word
oui	west
huit	you eat
fille	yes, see ya later

1

CONSONANT SOUNDS
Pronounced as in the

French word	English word
bonne	bun
dans	dog
fou	first, pharmacy
garçon	go
je	measure
chose	shake
café, qui	cap, kennel
le	let
mette	met
nette	net
montagne	canyon, onion, union
père	pear
rose	rose
si	see
te	lot
vous	vine
zèbre	zebra
ça	sorry

- If you can, give equal stress to all syllables in a French word; do not raise your voice on any particular syllable.
- If you can't give equal stress to all syllables in a French word, then raise your voice slightly on the last syllable.

    EXAMPLES:
    chapeau (shah-PO), *magazine* (mah-gah-ZEEN), *perspicacité* (per-spee-kah-see-TAY)

- Do not pronounce the last letter of a French word if it is a consonant.

    EXAMPLES:
    beaucoup (bo-KOO), *aéroport* (ah-air-o-POR)

Some common exceptions: *parc* (pARK), *chef* (shEFF), *avec* (ah-VEK). If you're not sure, don't pronounce the last consonant at all.

Mnemonic tip   If you don't know which is *accent aigu*
(acute) *(é)* and which is *accent grave (è)*,
remember that the patient died of acute ap-
pendicitis *(é)* and ended up in the grave *(è)*.

§2.

Capitalization, Punctuation Marks, and Word Division

§2.1 CAPITALIZATION

Generally speaking, do not capitalize days of the week, months of the year, languages, adjectives of nationality, and religions.

dimanche, lundi, mardi, etc.; janvier, février, mars, etc.; français, espagnol, anglais, etc.; Antonio est italien, María est espagnole; Pierre est français; Jacques est catholique.

Nouns of nationality are capitalized.
un Américain / an American (male);
une Française / a French woman.

§2.2 PUNCTUATION MARKS

The basic punctuation marks in French are:

le point / period   .
point virgule / semicolon   ;
la virgule / comma   ,
l'apostrophe (f) / apostrophe   '
deux points / colon   :
les parenthèses (f) / parentheses   ( )
les guillemets (m) / quotation marks   « »
le point d'interrogation / question mark   ?
les points de suspension / ellipses points   . . .

4

§2.3 WORD DIVISION

It is good to know how to divide a word into syllables (not only in French but also in English) because it helps you pronounce and spell the word correctly.

Basic Rules

- A syllable must contain a vowel, but it may contain only one vowel and no consonant.

    é / cole (*école* / school)

- When you are dealing with single separate consonants, each consonant remains with the vowel that follows it.

    beau / coup (*beaucoup* / many, much)

- When two consonants come together, they are separated; the first remains with the preceding syllable and the second remains with the following syllable.

    im / por / tant (*important*)

But if the second of the two consonants that come together is *l* or *r*, do not separate them:

a / près (*après* / after); *im / meu / ble* (*immeuble* / apartment building)

- When three consonants come together, the first two remain with the preceding vowel and the third remains with the vowel that follows it.

    ins / ti / tut (*institut*)

But if the third of the three consonants is *l* or *r*, do not separate that third consonant from the second; it remains with the second consonant.

com / pren / dre (*comprendre* / to understand)

Vowels

- Two vowels together are generally separated if they are strong vowels *(a, e, o)*.

  a /é /ro /port (*aéroport* / airport)

But if you are dealing with a weak vowel *(i, u)*, it ordinarily remains in the same syllable with its neighboring vowel, especially if that other vowel is a strong vowel.

  huî /tre (*huître* / oyster)

The Parts of Speech

3.

Articles

3.1 DEFINITE ARTICLE

The definite article in French has four forms, and they all mean "the":

Gender	Singular	Plural
Masculine	*le, l'*	*les*
Feminine	*la, l'*	*les*

Singular	Plural
le garçon / the boy	*les garçons* / the boys
l'arbre (m) / the tree	*les arbres* / the trees
la jeune fille / the girl	*les jeunes filles* / the girls
l'actrice / the actress	*les actrices* / the actresses

Definite Article Used

WITH NOUNS

- Before each noun even when more than one noun is stat

    J'ai le livre et le cahier. / I have the book and notebook.

- When you make a general statement.

    J'aime le lait. / I like milk.
    J'aime l'été. / I like summer.

- With a noun of weight or measure to express "a," "an,"
"per."

    dix francs la livre / ten francs a pound
    vingt francs la douzaine / twenty francs a dozen

- Before a noun indicating a profession, rank, or title follow
by the name of the person.

    Le professeur Poulin est absent aujourd'hui. / Professor Poul
    is absent today.

- With the name of a language.

    J'étudie le français. / I'm studying French.

    EXCEPTION: Do *not* use the definite article when the name
    of a language directly follows a form of the verb *parler.*

    Je parle français et russe. / I speak French and Russian.

- With the days of the week to indicate an action that is
habitually repeated.

    Le samedi je vais au cinéma. / On Saturdays I go to the movi

    But when you want to indicate a *particular* day, do not us
    the definite article.

    Samedi je vais au cinéma. / Saturday I am going to the movie
    (understood: this Saturday)

With parts of the body or articles of clothing if the possessor is clearly stated.

Luigi, qui est italien, a les cheveux noirs. / Luigi, who is Italian, has black hair.

With family names in the plural, in which case the spelling of the family name does not change.

Nous allons chez les Durand. / We're going to the Durands.

WITH PREPOSITIONS

When the prepositions *à* and *de* come before the definite article, it contracts as follows:

Preposition		Article		Contraction
à	+	le	>	*au*
	+	les	>	*aux*
de	+	le	>	*du*
	+	les	>	*des*

But there is *no* change with *l'* or *la*.

Je vais à l'aéroport. / I'm going to the airport.
Je vais à la bibliothèque. / I'm going to the library.
Je viens de l'aéroport. / I'm coming from the airport.
Je viens de la bibliothèque. / I'm coming from the library.

With the preposition *à* (which combines to form *au* or *aux*) in front of the name of a country that is masculine.

Nous allons au Canada / We're going to Canada.
Janine vient aux États-Unis. / Janine is coming to the United States.

With the preposition *de* (which combines to form *du* or *des*) before the name of a country that is masculine.

> *du Portugal* / from Portugal
> *des Etats-Unis* / from the United States

With the preposition *de* + a common noun to indicate possession.

> *le livre du garçon* / the boy's book
> *les livres des garçons* / the boys' books
> *la robe de la jeune fille* / the girl's dress
> *les poupées des petites filles* / the little girls' dolls

WITH CERTAIN EXPRESSIONS

• Indicating segments of the day.

> *l'après-midi* / in the afternoon; *le matin* / in the morning;
> *le soir* / in the evening

• Common expressions.

> *à l'école* / to school, in school; *à la maison* / at home
> *la semaine dernière* / last week; *l'année dernière* / last year
> *la plupart de* / most of
> *la plupart des jeunes filles* / most of the girls

• As a partitive in the affirmative.

> *J'ai du café.* / I have (some) coffee.
> *Tu as de l'argent.* / You have (some) money.
> *Il a des amis.* / He has friends.

Definite Article Not Used

However, the definite article is *not* used when the partitive is in the negative or when the definite article is used with an adjective.

Je n'ai pas de café. / I haven't any coffee.
Tu n'as pas d'argent. / You haven't any money.
Il a de bons amis. / He has some good friends.

Do not use the definite article:

In direct address: *Bonjour, docteur Leduc.*

After the preposition *en*: *Nous écrivons en français.* Exceptions:

> *en l'air* / in the air; *en l'absence de* / in the absence of
> *en l'honneur de* / in honor of

After the preposition *de* in an adjective phrase: *J'aime mon livre de français.*

With a feminine country and continents when you use *en* / at, to or *de* / of, from.

> *Je vais en France, en Angleterre, en Allemagne, en Australie, en Asie, et en Amérique.*
> *Paul vient de France, les Armstrong viennent d'Australie et Hilda vient d'Allemagne.*

With most cities: *à Paris, à New York; de Londres, de Montréal, de Sydney.*

With a noun in apposition: *Paul, fils du professeur Leblanc, est très aimable.*

With titles of monarchs:

> *Louis Seize (Louis XVI)* / Louis the Sixteenth

With the preposition *sans* or with the construction *ne . . . ni . . . ni . . . :*

> *Je n'ai ni papier ni stylo.* / I have neither paper nor pen.
> *Il est parti sans argent.* / He left without money.

With certain expressions of quantity that take *de: beaucoup de, trop de, combien de, peu de, plus de, assez de*

With the preposition *avec* when the noun after it is abstract:

> *Jean-Luc parle avec enthousiasme.*

§3.2 INDEFINITE ARTICLE

The forms of the indefinite article are:

> Singular
> *J'ai* **un** *frère.* / I have a brother.
> *J'ai* **une** *sœur.* / I have a sister.
>
> Plural
> *J'ai* **des** *frères.* / I have brothers.
> *J'ai* **des** *sœurs.* / I have sisters.

The indefinite article is used:

- When you want to say ''a'' or ''an.'' It is also used as a numeral to mean ''one'':

    un livre / a book or one book
    une orange / an orange or one orange

- In front of each noun in a series:

    J'ai un cahier, un crayon et une gomme. / I have a notebook, pencil, and eraser.

- With *C'est* or *Ce sont* with or without an adjective:

    C'est un docteur. / He's a doctor.
    C'est un mauvais docteur. / He's a bad doctor.
    Ce sont des étudiants. / They are students.

The indefinite article is *not* used:

- With *cent* and *mille:*

    J'ai cent dollars. / I have a hundred dollars.
    J'ai mille dollars. / I have a thousand dollars.

- With *il est, ils sont, elle est, elles sont* + an unmodified noun of nationality, profession, or religion:

    Elle est professeur. / She is a professor.
    Il est catholique. / He is (a) Catholic.

When you use *quel* in an exclamation:

> *Quelle femme!* / What a woman!
> *Quel homme!* / What a man!

With negations, particularly with the verb *avoir*:

> *Avez-vous un livre? Non, je n'ai pas de livre.* / Have you a
> book? No, I don't have a book (any book).

§3.3 PARTITIVE

The partitive denotes a *part* of a whole; in other words,
some. In English, we express the partitive by saying
"some" or "any" in front of the noun. Use the following
forms in front of the noun:

> Masculine singular: *du* or *de l'*
> Feminine singular: *de la* or *de l'*
> Masculine or feminine plural: *des*

Simple Affirmative

> *J'ai **du** café.* / I have some coffee.
> *J'ai **de la** viande.* / I have some meat.
> *J'ai **de l'**eau.* / I have some water.
> *J'ai **des** bonbons.* / I have some candy.

Simple Negative

> *Je **n'**ai **pas de** café.* / I don't have any coffee.
> *Je **n'**ai **pas de** viande.* / I don't have any meat.
> *Je **n'**ai **pas d'**eau.* / I don't have any water.
> *Je **n'**ai **pas de** bonbons.* / I don't have any candy.

With an Adjective

> *J'ai **de jolis** chapeaux.* / I have some pretty hats.
> *J'ai **de jolies** robes.* / I have some pretty dresses.

Note the following:
- When the noun is preceded by an adverb or noun of quantity or measure, use *de,* as in *J'ai beaucoup de choses.* I have many things.
- When the noun is modified by another noun, use *de,* as in *une école de filles.*
- The partitive is not used with *sans* or *ne . . . ni . . . ni.*

  EXAMPLE:
  J'ai quitté la maison sans argent. / I left the house without any money.

- Use *quelques* and not the partitive when by "some" you mean "a few," in other words, "not many."

  EXAMPLES:
  J'ai quelques amis. / I have a few (some) friends.
  J'ai quelques bonbons. / I have a few (some) candies.

- When the negated verb is *ne . . . que* / only, the partitive consists of *de* plus the definite article.

  EXAMPLES:
  Elle ne lit que des livres. / She reads only books.
  Elle ne mange que des bonbons. / She eats only candy.

- The partitive must be repeated before each noun.

  EXAMPLE:
  Ici on vend du papier, de l'encre et des cahiers. / Here they sell paper, ink, and notebooks.

Nouns

§4.1 GENERAL

A *noun* is a word that refers to a person, place, thing, or quality. Nouns are either masculine or feminine and require the article *le, la, l'*, or *les*. The gender of nouns that refer to persons or animals is obvious.

Examples

PERSONS	
Masculine	**Feminine**
l'homme / the man	*la femme* / the woman
le garçon / the boy	*la jeune fille* / the girl
l'oncle / the uncle	*la tante* / the aunt

ANIMALS	
Masculine	**Feminine**
le taureau / the bull	*la vache* / the cow
le coq / the rooster	*la poule* / the hen
le chat / the cat	*la chatte* / the cat

The gender of nouns referring to anything other than persons or animals must be learned with the noun.

Examples

Gender	Noun Endings	Examples
Masculine	*-age* or *-âge*	*l'âge* / age
		le fromage / cheese
	-ment	*le logement* / lodging
		le médicament / medicine (you take)
	-eau	*le chapeau* / hat
		le gâteau / cake
Feminine	*-ance*	*la circonstance* / circumstance
		la chance / chance, luck
	-ence	*l'apparence* / appearance
		la science / science
	-tion	*l'attention* / attention
		la notion / idea, notion
	-ette	*la fourchette* / fork
		la serviette / napkin
		la sucette / lollipop

Special Cases

Some nouns have one meaning when masculine, another meaning when feminine:

Masculine	**Feminine**
le livre / book	*la livre* / pound
le tour / turn	*la tour* / tower

Some nouns are the same for both:

Masculine	**Feminine**
un élève / pupil (boy)	*une élève* / pupil (girl)
un enfant / child (boy)	*une enfant* / child (girl)

Some nouns add *-e* to the masculine to form the feminine:

Masculine	**Feminine**
un cousin / cousin	*une cousine* / cousin
un ami / friend	*une amie* / friend

Some nouns change the *-eur* masculine ending to *-euse* for feminine:

Masculine
un vendeur / salesman
un menteur / liar

Feminine
une vendeuse / saleswoman
une menteuse / liar

§4.2 PLURAL OF NOUNS—THE BASICS

Add *-s* to the singular:

Singular	Plural
le livre / the book	*les livres* / the books
la maison / the house	*les maisons* / the houses
l'étudiant / the student	*les étudiants* / the students

If a noun ends in *-s, -x,* or *-z* in the singular, leave it alone:

Singular	Plural
le bras / the arm	*les bras* / the arms
la voix / the voice	*les voix* / the voices
le nez / the nose	*les nez* / the noses

If a noun ends in *-al* in the singular, change *-al* to *-aux:*

Singular
le journal / the newspaper
Plural
les journaux / the newspapers

If a noun ends in *-eu* or *-eau* in the singular, add *-x*:

> **Singular**
> *le feu* / the fire
> *le bureau* / the office, the desk
>
> **Plural**
> *les feux* / the fires
> *les bureaux* / the offices, desks

Common irregular nouns

Singular	Plural
le ciel / the sky	*les cieux* / the skies
l'œil / the eye	*les yeux* / the eyes

Adjectives

5.1 FORMATION

Feminine Singular

The feminine singular of an adjective is normally formed by adding -e to the masculine singular.

EXAMPLES
joli — jolie / pretty   *présent — présente* / present
grand — grande / tall

If a masculine singular adjective already ends in -e, the feminine singular is the same form.

EXAMPLES
aimable / kind   *énorme* / huge   *faible* / weak

Some feminine singular forms are irregular. If a masculine singular adjective ends in -c, change it to -que for the feminine; -er to -ère; -f to -ve; -g to -gue; and -x to -se.

EXAMPLES
public — publique / public   *long — longue* / long
premier — première / first   *heureux — heureuse* / happy
actif — active / active

Some masculine singular adjectives double the final consonant before adding -e to form the feminine.

EXAMPLES
ancien — ancienne / old   *cruel — cruelle* / cruel
bas — basse / low   *gentil — gentille* / kind, nice
bon — bonne / good

- The following feminine singular adjectives are formed fr the irregular masculine singular forms:

Masculine Singular Before a Masculine Singular Noun Beginning with a Consonant	Irregular Masculine Singular Before a Masculine Singular Noun Beginning with Vowel or Silent *H*
beau / beautiful, handsome	*bel ami*
fou / crazy	*fol ami*
nouveau / new	*nouvel hôtel*
vieux / old	*vieil ami*

Feminine Singular
belle amie
folle amie
nouvelle amie
vieille amie

> **Mnemonic tip** *La vieille dame a passé la veille de Noë avec son vieil ami dans un vieux cabare* The old lady spent Christmas Eve with old friend in an old cabaret.

- Some common masculine singular adjectives have irreg forms in the feminine singular. These do not fall into any particular category like those above.

EXAMPLES

blanc—blanche / white
complet—complète / complete
doux—douce / soft, smooth, sweet
faux—fausse / false

favori—favorite / favorite
frais—fraîche / fres
sec—sèche / dry

Plural

The plural is normally formed by adding *-s* to the masculine or feminine singular.

EXAMPLES
bon — bons; bonne — bonnes / good *joli — jolis; jolie — jolies* / pretty

If the masculine singular already ends in *-s* or *-x*, it remains the same in the masculine plural.

EXAMPLES
gris — gris / gray   *heureux — heureux* /happy

If a masculine singular adjective ends in *-al*, it changes to *-aux* (with some exceptions).

EXAMPLES
égal — égaux / equal   *principal — principaux* / principal

If a masculine singular adjective ends in *-eau,* it changes to *-eaux.*

EXAMPLE
nouveau — nouveaux / new

§5.2 AGREEMENT

An adjective agrees in gender (feminine or masculine) and number (singular or plural) with the noun or pronoun it modifies.

EXAMPLES:
Alexandre et Théodore sont beaux et intelligents. / Alexander and Theodore are handsome and smart.
Yolande est belle. / Yolande is beautiful.
Janine et Monique sont belles. / Janine and Monique are beautiful.
Hélène et Simone sont actives. / Helene and Simone are active.

Anne est jolie. / Anne is pretty.
C'est un bel arbre. / It is a beautiful tree.
Ils sont amusants. / They are amusing.
Chaque garçon est présent. / Every boy is here (present).
Chaque jeune fille est présente. / Every girl is here (present).
Valentine est absente. / Valentine is absent.

§5.3 POSITION

- In French, most descriptive adjectives are placed after the noun; e.g., colors, nationality, religion: *une robe blanche* / white dress, *un fromage français* / a French cheese, *une femme catholique* / a Catholic woman

- Here are some examples of common short adjectives that are generally placed in front of the noun:

    un autre livre / another book, *un bel arbre* / a beautiful tree, *un beau cadeau* / a beautiful gift, *un bon dîner* / a good dinner, *chaque jour* / each day, *un gros livre* / a big book, *une jeune dame* / a young lady, *une jolie maison* / a pretty house, *une petite table* / a small table, *plusieurs amis* / several friends, *un vieil homme* / an old man, *le premier rang* / the first row, *quelques bonbons* / some candy, *un tel garçon* / such a boy, *toute la journée* / all day.

- Some adjectives change in meaning, depending on whether the adjective is in front of the noun or after it. The most common are:

la semaine dernière / last week	*la dernière semaine* / the last (final) week
ma robe propre / my clean dress	*ma propre robe* / my own dress
une femme brave / a brave woman	*une brave femme* / a fine woman
le même moment / the same moment	*le moment même* / the very moment
un livre cher / an expensive book	*un cher ami* / a dear friend

§5.4 TYPES

§5.4–1 Descriptive

A descriptive adjective is a word that describes a noun or pronoun: *une belle maison* / a beautiful house, *un beau livre* / a beautiful book, *un bel arbre* / a beautiful tree, *une jolie femme* / a pretty woman.

Elle est grande. / She is tall.

§5.4–2 Demonstrative

A demonstrative adjective is used to point out something or someone.

Gender	Singular	Plural
Masculine	*ce, cet* / this, that	*ces* / these, those
Feminine	*cette* / this, that	*ces* / these, those

EXAMPLES:
Ce garçon est beau. / This boy is handsome.
Cet arbre est beau. / This tree is beautiful.
Cette femme est belle. / This woman is beautiful.
Ces hommes sont beaux. / These men are handsome.
Ces livres sont beaux. / These books are beautiful.
Ces dames sont belles. / These ladies are beautiful.

If you wish to make a contrast between "this" and "that" or "these" and "those," add *-ci* this, these or *-là* that, those to the noun with a hyphen.

Ce garçon-ci est plus fort que ce garçon-là. / This boy is stronger than that boy.

The form *cet* is used in front of a masculine singular noun or adjective beginning with a vowel or silent *h: cet arbre, cet homme.*

If there is more than one noun, a demonstrative adjective must be used in front of each noun: *cette dame et ce monsieur*.

§5.4–3 Interrogative

The adjective *quel* is generally regarded as interrogative because it is frequently used in a question. Its forms are *quel, quelle, quels, quelles*.

EXAMPLES:
Quel livre voulez-vous? / Which book do you want?
Quel est votre nom? / What is your name?
Quelle heure est-il? / What time is it?
Quelle est votre adresse? / What is your address?
Quels sont les mois de l'année? / What are the months of the year?
Quelles sont les saisons? / What are the seasons?

The adjective *quel* is also used in exclamations. Note that the indefinite article *un (une)* is not used in this case.

EXAMPLES
Quel garçon! / What a boy!
Quelle jeune fille! / What a girl!

§5.4–4 Possessive

MASCULINE	
Singular	**Plural**
mon livre / my book	*mes livres* / my books
ton stylo / your pen	*tes stylos* / your pens
son ballon / his (her, its) balloon	*ses ballons* / his (her, its) balloons
notre parapluie / our umbrella	*nos parapluies* / our umbrellas
votre sandwich / your sandwich	*vos sandwichs* / your sandwiches
leur gâteau / their cake	*leurs gâteaux* / their cakes

FEMININE	
Singular	**Plural**
ma robe / my dress	*mes robes* / my dresses
ta jaquette / your jacket	*tes jaquettes* / your jackets
sa balle / his (her, its) ball	*ses balles* / his (her, its) balls
notre maison / our house	*nos maisons* / our houses
votre voiture / your car	*vos voitures* / your cars
leur sœur / their sister	*leurs sœurs* / their sisters

- A possessive adjective agrees in gender and number with the noun it modifies.

- *Notre, votre,* and *leur* do not agree with the gender of the noun in the singular. They are all the same, whether in front of a masculine or feminine singular noun.

- Possessive adjectives do not agree with the gender of the noun in the plural. They are all the same, whether in front of a masculine or feminine plural noun: *mes, tes, ses, nos, vos, leurs.*

- Be aware of *mon (ma), ton (ta), son (sa):* In front of a feminine singular noun beginning with a vowel or silent *h*, the masculine singular forms are used: *mon, ton, son* — not *ma, ta, sa.*

> *mon adresse* / my address
> *ton opinion* / your opinion
> *son amie* / his (or her) friend
> *mon habitude* / my habit (custom)

- Since *son, sa,* and *ses* can mean ''his'' or ''her,'' you may add *à lui* or *à elle* to make the meaning clear.

> *sa maison à lui* / his house
> *sa maison à elle* / her house
> *son livre à lui* / his book
> *son livre à elle* / her book
> *ses livres à lui* / his books
> *ses livres à elle* / her books

- If there is more than one noun, a possessive adjective must be used in front of each noun: *ma mère et mon père, mon livre et mon cahier.*

Possessive Adjectives with Parts of the Body and Clothing

- When using the verb *avoir,* the definite article is normally used with parts of the body, **not** the possessive adjective.

    Henri a les mains sales. / Henry has dirty hands.
    Simone a les cheveux roux. / Simone has red hair.

- When using a reflexive verb, the definite article is normally used, **not** the possessive adjective.

    Paulette s'est lavé les cheveux. / Paulette washed her hair.

- The *definite article* is used instead of the possessive adjective when referring to parts of the body or clothing if it is clear who the possessor is.

    Henri tient le livre dans la main. / Henry is holding the book in his hand.

§5.4–5 Comparative and Superlative

Comparative

Of the same degree: *aussi . . . que* / as . . . as
Of a lesser degree: *moins . . . que* / less . . . than
Of a higher degree: *plus . . . que* / more . . . than

Janine est aussi grande que Monique. / Janine is as tall as
  Monique.
Monique est moins intelligente que Janine. / Monique is less
  intelligent than Janine.
Janine est plus jolie que Monique. / Janine is prettier than
  Monique.

- *Aussi . . . que* becomes *si . . . que* in a negative sentence.

  Robert n'est pas si grand que Joseph. / Robert is not as tall as
  Joseph.

The comparative forms of the adjective "bad" are *mauvais,
pire, le pire.*

  Ce crayon est mauvais. / This pencil is bad.
  Ce crayon est pire que l'autre. / This pencil is worse than the
  other.
  Ce crayon est le pire. / This pencil is the worst.

- *Plus que* / more than becomes *plus de* + a number.

  EXAMPLES
  Il a plus de cinquante ans. / He is more than fifty years old.
  Je lui ai donné plus de cent dollars. / I gave him (her) more than
  a hundred dollars.

Superlative

- The superlative is formed by placing the appropriate definite
  article *(le, la, les)* in front of the comparative:

  Marie est la plus jolie jeune fille de la classe. / Mary is the
  prettiest girl in the class.

- If the adjective normally follows the noun, the definite article
  must be used twice—in front of the noun and in front of
  the superlative:

  Monsieur Hibou fut le président le plus sage de la nation. / Mr.
  Hibou was the wisest president of the nation.

- After a superlative, the preposition *de* (not *dans*) is normally used to express "in":

    Pierre est le plus beau garçon de la classe. / Peter is the most handsome boy in the class.

- If more than one comparative or superlative is expressed, each is repeated:

    Marie est la plus intelligente et la plus sérieuse de l'école. / Mary is the most intelligent and most serious in the school.

> *Une devinette* (a riddle) using a superlative:
>
> *Quelle est la chose la plus sale de la maison?* / What is the dirtiest thing in the house?
>
> *un balai* / a broom

Irregular Comparative and Superlative Adjectives

Adjective (m)	Comparative	Superlative
bon / good	*meilleur* / better	*le meilleur* / (the) best
mauvais / bad	*plus mauvais* ⎫ worse *pire* ⎭	*le plus mauvais* ⎫ (the) worst *le pire* ⎭
petit / small	*plus petit* / smaller (in size) *moindre* / less (in importance)	*le plus petit* / (the) smallest *le moindre* / (the) least

§5.4–6 *Meilleur* and *Mieux*

Meilleur is an adjective and must agree in gender and number with the noun or pronoun it modifies.

EXAMPLE

Cette pomme est bonne, cette pomme-là est meilleure que celle-ci et celle-là est la meilleure. / This apple is good, that apple is better than this one, and that one is the best.

Mieux is an adverb and does not change in form.

EXAMPLE

Marie chante bien, Anne chante mieux que Marie et Claire chante le mieux. / Mary sings well, Anne sings better than Mary, and Claire sings the best.

> **Mnemonic tip** The adverb *bien* / well and the adverb *mieux* / better both contain *ie*.

§5.4–7 Adjectives Used in an Adverbial Sense

An adjective used as an adverb does not normally change in form.

Cette rose sent bon. / This rose smells good.
Ces bonbons coûtent cher. / These candies are expensive.

§6.

Pronouns

§6.1 TYPES

§6.1–1 Subject Pronouns

The subject pronouns are:

Person	Singular	Plural
1st	*je (j')* / I	*nous* / we
2d	*tu* / you (familiar)	*vous* / you (singular polite or plural)
	il / he, it	
3d	*elle* / she, it	*ils* / they *(m.)*
	on / one	*elles* / they *(f.)*

- Note that *je* becomes *j'* before a vowel or a silent *h:*

  j'aime / I love; *j'hésite* / I hesitate.

- Remember that *vous* is not always plural; it is also the polite form of the second person; *tu* is the familiar form. You can use the *tu* form with members of the family and close friends, but always use the *vous* form with strangers and with people you do not know well.

§6.1–2 Direct Object Pronouns

The direct object pronouns are:

Person	Singular
1st	*me (m')* / me
2d	*te (t')* / you (familiar)
3d	*le (l')* / him, it *la (l')* / her, it (person or thing)

Person	Plural
1st	*nous* / us
2d	*vous* / you (singular polite or plural)
3d	*les* / them (persons or things)

- A direct object pronoun takes the place of a direct object noun.

- A direct object noun ordinarily comes after the verb, but a direct object pronoun is ordinarily placed *in front* of the verb or infinitive.

    EXAMPLES
    J'ai les lettres. / I have the letters. → *Je les ai.* / I have them.
    Je connais Luigi. / I know Luigi. → *Je le connais.* / I know him.

Mnemonic tip	*Je lis la leçon.* / I'm reading the lesson.

    Drop the noun *leçon;* what remains is *la,* the feminine singular definite article. It now becomes the direct object pronoun. Place it in front of the verb: *Je la lis.* / I'm reading it.

- *Me, te, le,* and *la* become *m', t', l'* when directly followed by a verb that starts with a vowel or silent *h.*

§6.1–3 Indirect Object Pronouns

The indirect object pronouns are:

Person	Singular	
1st	*me (m')*	to me
2d	*te (t')*	to you (familiar)
3d	*lui*	to him, to her

Person	Plural	
1st	*nous*	to us
2d	*vous*	to you (singular polite or plural)
3d	*leur*	to them

- An indirect object pronoun takes the place of an indirect object noun.

- An indirect object pronoun is ordinarily placed *in front* of the verb.

    EXAMPLES
    Je parle à Janine. / I'm talking to Janine. → *Je lui parle.* / I'm talking to her.
    Je parle à Luigi et à mon ami. / I'm talking to Luigi and my friend. → *Je leur parle.* / I'm talking to them.

§6.1–4 Double Object Pronouns

To get a picture of what the word order is when you have more than one object pronoun (direct and indirect) in a sentence, see Word Order of Elements in French Sentences, §11.

§6.1–5 *En*

• The pronoun *en* takes the place of the partitive and serves as a direct object. It can refer to persons or things.

> EXAMPLES
> *Avez-vous des frères?* / Do you have any brothers?
> *Oui, j'en ai.* / Yes, I have (some).
> *Avez-vous de l'argent?* / Have you any money?
> *Oui, j'en ai.* / Yes, I have (some). *Non, je n'en ai pas.* / No, I don't have any.

• The past participle of a compound verb does not agree with the preceding direct object *en*.

> *Avez-vous écrit des lettres?* / Did you write any letters?
> *Oui, j'en ai écrit trois.* / Yes, I wrote three (of them).

• When using a reflexive verb, use *en* to take the place of the preposition *de* + a thing.

> *Est-ce que vous vous souvenez de l'adresse?* / Do you remember the address?
> *Oui, je m'en souviens.* / Yes, I remember it.
>
> *Est-ce que vous prenez des hors-d'œuvre?* / Are you helping yourself to the hors d'œuvre?
> *Oui, merci, j'en prends.* / Yes, thank you, I'm helping myself to some.

Do not use *en* to take the place of the preposition *de* + a person. Use a disjunctive pronoun (see §6.1 – 7).

> *Est-ce que vous vous souvenez de cette dame?* / Do you remember this lady?
> *Oui, je me souviens d'elle.* / Yes, I remember her.

• Use *en* to take the place of *de* + noun and retain the word of quantity.

> *Avez-vous beaucoup d'amis?* / Do you have many friends?
> *Oui, j'en ai beaucoup.* / Yes, I have many (of them).

Madame Paquet a-t-elle mis trop de sel dans le ragoût? / Did Mrs. Paquet put too much salt in the stew?
Oui, elle en a mis trop dans le ragoût. / Yes, she put too much (of it) in the stew.

- Use *en* to take the place of the preposition *de* + the place to mean "from there."

Est-ce que vous venez de l'école? / Are you coming from school?
Oui, j'en viens. / Yes, I'm coming from there.
Non, je n'en viens pas. / No, I am not coming from there.

§6.1–6 Y

Use *y* as a pronoun to serve as an object replacing a prepositional phrase beginning with *à, dans, sur,* or *chez* that refers to things, places, or ideas.

Est-ce que vous pensez à l'examen? / Are you thinking of the exam?
Oui, j'y pense. / Yes, I'm (thinking of it).

Je réponds à la lettre. / I'm answering the letter.
J'y réponds. / I'm answering it.

Est-ce que les fleurs sont sur la table? / Are the flowers on the table?
Oui, elles y sont. / Yes, they are (there).

Est-ce que vous allez chez Pierre? / Are you going to Pierre's?
Oui, j'y vais. / Yes, I'm going (there).

§6.1–7 Disjunctive Pronouns

Person	Singular		Plural	
1st	*moi*	me, I	*nous*	us, we
2nd	*toi*	you (familiar)	*vous*	you (formal singular or plural)
3rd	*soi*	oneself	*eux*	them, they (m.)
	lui	him, he	*elles*	them, they (f.)
	elle	her, she		

Mnemonic tip

Je vais chez moi. / I'm going to my house.
Tu vas chez toi. / You're going to your house.
Il va chez lui. / He's going to his house.
Elle va chez elle. / She's going to her house.
On va chez soi. / One is going to one's own house.

Nous allons chez nous. / We're going to our house.
Vous allez chez vous. / You're going to your house.
Ils vont chez eux. / They're going to their house.
Elles vont chez elles. / They're going to their house.

A disjunctive pronoun is used:

• as object of a preposition.

Elle parle avec moi. / She is talking with me.
Je pense toujours à toi. / I always think of you.

in a compound subject or object.

Elle et lui sont amoureux. / He and she are in love.
Je vous connais — toi et lui. / I know you — you and him.

for emphasis.

Moi, je parle bien; lui, il ne parle pas bien. / I speak well; he
does not speak well.

to indicate possession with *à* if the verb is *être* and if the
subject is a noun, personal pronoun, or demonstrative
pronoun.

Ce livre est à moi. / This book is mine.
Je suis à toi. / I am yours.

with *c'est* and *ce sont.*

Qui est à la porte? — C'est moi. / Who is at the door? It is I.
C'est toi? Oui, c'est moi. / Is it you? Yes, it is I.

Est-ce que ce sont eux?—Oui, ce sont eux. / Is it they?—Yes, it's they.

- with *même* and *mêmes*.

  Est-ce Pierre?—Oui, c'est lui-même. / Is it Peter? Yes, it's he himself.
  Vont-ils les manger eux-mêmes? / Are they going to eat them themselves?

- when no verb is stated.

  Qui est à l'appareil? Moi. / Who is on the phone? I (am).
  Qui a brisé le vase? Eux. / Who broke the vase? They (did).

See also Order of Elements in French Sentences, §11.

§6.1–8 Demonstrative Pronouns

The demonstrative pronouns are:

	Singular	**Plural**
Masculine	*celui* / the one	*ceux* / the ones
Feminine	*celle* / the one	*celles* / the ones

EXAMPLES
J'ai mangé mon gâteau et celui de Pierre. / I ate my cake and Peter's.
Il aime beaucoup ma voiture et celle de Jacques. / He likes my car very much and Jack's.
J'ai mangé mes petits pois et ceux de David. / I ate my peas and David's.
J'aime tes jupes et celles de Jeanne. / I like your skirts and Joan's.
J'ai deux éclairs; est-ce que tu préfères celui-ci ou celui-là? / I have two eclairs; do you prefer this one or that one?
J'ai deux pommes; est-ce que tu préfères celle-ci ou celle-là? / I have two apples; do you prefer this one or that one?

Une devinette / a riddle

J'ai un chapeau, mais je n'ai pas de tête. Ne trouvez-vous pas que c'est bête? / I have a hat, but I don't have a head. Don't you think it's stupid?

un champignon / a mushroom

ce (c'), ceci, cela, ça

These are demonstrative pronouns but they are invariable; that is, they do not change in gender and number. They refer to things that are not identified by name and may refer to an idea or a statement mentioned.

EXAMPLES
C'est vrai. / It's true.
Ceci est vrai. / This is true. *Ceci est faux.* / This is false.
Cela est vrai. / That is true. *Cela est faux.* / That is false.
Ça m'intéresse beaucoup. / That interests me very much.
Qu'est-ce que c'est que cela? OR *Qu'est-ce que c'est que ça?* / What's that?
Note that *cela* shortens to *ça*.

§6.1–9 Indefinite Pronouns

aucun (aucune) / not any, not one, none
un autre (une autre) / another, another one
nous autres Français / we French (people)
nous autres Américains / we American (people)
certains (certaines) / certain ones
chacun (chacune) / each one
nul (nulle) / not one, not any, none
n'importe qui, n'importe quel / anyone
n'importe quoi / anything
on / people, one, they, you, we

   On dit qu'il va pleuvoir. / They say that it's going to rain.

personne / no one, nobody
plusieurs / several

> *J'en ai plusieurs.* / I have several (of them).

quelque chose / something
quelqu'un (quelqu'une) / someone, somebody
quelques-uns (quelques-unes) / some, a few
quiconque / whoever, whosoever
soi / oneself

> *On est chez soi dans cet hôtel.* / People feel at home in this hotel.

tout / all, everything

> *Tout est bien qui finit bien.* / All is well that ends well.

§6.1–10 Interrogative Pronouns

Referring to Persons

- As subject of a verb:

> *Qui est à l'appareil?* / Who is on the phone?
> *Qui est-ce qui est à l'appareil?* / Who is on the phone?
> *Lequel des deux garçons arrive?* / Which (one) of the two boys is arriving?
> *Laquelle des deux jeunes filles est ici?* / Which (one) of the two girls is here?

- As direct object of a verb:

> *Qui aimez-vous?* / Whom do you love?
> *Qui est-ce que vous aimez?* / Whom do you love?
> *Lequel de ces deux garçons aimez-vous?* / Which (one) of these two boys do you love?
> *Laquelle de ces deux jeunes filles aimez-vous?* / Which (one) of these two girls do you love?

- As object of a preposition:

> *Avec qui allez-vous au cinéma?* / With whom are you going to the movies?

A qui parlez-vous au téléphone? / To whom are you talking on the telephone?

Note that when the interrogative pronouns *lequel (laquelle), lesquels (lesquelles)* are objects of the prepositions *à* or *de,* their forms are:

Singular	**Plural**
auquel (à laquelle)	*auxquels (auxquelles)*
duquel (de laquelle)	*desquels (desquelles)*

Auquel de ces deux garçons parlez-vous? / To which (one) of these two boys are you talking?
A laquelle de ces deux jeunes filles parlez-vous? / To which (one) of these two girls are you talking?
Auxquels de ces hommes parlez-vous? / To which (ones) of these men do you talk?
Auxquelles de ces femmes parlez-vous? / To which (ones) of these women are you talking?
Duquel de ces deux garçons parlez-vous? / About which (one) of these two boys are you talking?

Referring to Things

As subject of a verb:

Qu'est-ce qui est arrivé? / What arrived? OR What happened?
Qu'est-ce qui s'est passé? / What happened?

Une devinette avec qu'est-ce qui

Qu'est-ce qui vous appartient et dont les autres se servent souvent? / What belongs to you that others use often?

votre nom / your name

Laquelle de ces deux voitures marche bien? / Which (one) of these two cars runs well?
Lesquels de tous ces trains sont modernes? / Which (ones) of all these trains are modern?

● As direct object of a verb:

> *Que faites-vous?* / What are you doing?
> *Qu'a-t-elle?* / What does she have? OR What's the matter wi
> her?
> *Qu'est-ce que vous faites?* / What are you doing?
> *Laquelle de ces voitures préférez-vous?* / Which (one) of thes
> cars do you prefer?

● As object of a preposition:

> *Avec quoi écrivez-vous?* / With what are you writing?
> *A quoi pensez-vous?* / Of what are you thinking? OR What ar
> you thinking of?

§6.1–11 Possessive Pronouns

MASCULINE			
Singular		**Plural**	
le mien	mine	*les miens*	mine
le tien	yours (familiar)	*les tiens*	yours (familia
le sien	his, hers, its	*les siens*	his, hers, its
le nôtre	ours	*les nôtres*	ours
le vôtre	yours	*les vôtres*	yours
le leur	theirs	*les leurs*	theirs

FEMININE			
Singular		**Plural**	
la mienne	mine	*les miennes*	mine
la tienne	yours (familiar)	*les tiennes*	yours (familia
la sienne	his, hers, its	*les siennes*	his, hers, its
la nôtre	ours	*les nôtres*	ours
la vôtre	yours	*les vôtres*	yours
la leur	theirs	*les leurs*	theirs

● A possessive pronoun takes the place of a possessive
adjective + noun.

> *mon livre* / my book; *le mien* / mine.

A possessive pronoun agrees in gender and number with what it is replacing.

son livre / his (her) book; *le sien* / his (hers).

When the definite articles *le* and *les* are preceded by the prepositions *à* and *de,* they combine as follows: *au mien, aux miens, du mien, des miens.*

Paul me parle de ses parents et je lui parle des miens. / Paul is talking to me about his parents and I am talking to him about mine.
Je préfère ma voiture à la tienne. / I prefer my car to yours.

Possessive pronouns are used with *être* to emphasize a distinction.

Ce livre-ci est le mien et celui-là est le tien. / This book is mine and that one is yours.

If no distinction is made as to who owns what, use *être* + *à* + disjunctive pronoun.

Ce livre est à lui. / This book is his.

Instead of using the possessive pronouns in French, we say "one of my friends," "one of my books," etc.

un de mes amis / a friend of mine; *un de mes livres* / a book of mine
une de ses amies / a girlfriend of his (hers)
un de nos amis / a friend of ours

§6.1–12 Reflexive Pronouns

The reflexive pronouns, which are used with reflexive verbs, are *me, te, se, nous,* and *vous.*

The corresponding English pronouns are: myself, yourself, herself, himself, oneself, itself, ourselves, yourselves, themselves.

- To form the present tense of a reflexive verb in a simple affirmative sentence, put the reflexive pronoun in front of the verb.

    Je me lave. / I wash myself.

- A reflexive verb expresses an action that turns back upon the subject.

    Jacqueline se lave tous les jours. / Jacqueline washes herself every day.

You must be careful to use the appropriate reflexive pronoun—the one that matches the subject pronoun. You already know the subject pronouns, but here they are again, beside the reflexive pronouns.

Person	Singular	Plural
1st	*je me lave*	*nous nous lavons*
2d	*tu te laves*	*vous vous lavez*
3d	*il se lave* *elle se lave* *on se lave*	*ils se lavent* *elles se lavent*

To get a picture of what the word order is when you have more than one pronoun of any kind in a sentence, se Word Order of Elements in French Sentences (§11.).

§6.1–13 Relative Pronouns

A *relative pronoun* is a word that refers to an antecedent. An *antecedent* is something that comes before something it can be a word, a phrase, a clause that is replaced by a pronoun or some other substitute. For example, in the sentence ''Is it Mary who did that?'' ''who'' is the relative pronoun and "Mary" is the antecedent. Another example: "It seems to me that you are wrong, which is what I had suspected right along." The relative pronoun is "which" and the antecedent is the clause, "that you are wrong."

Some common relative pronouns are:

dont / of whom, of which, whose, whom, which

> *Voici le livre dont j'ai besoin.* / Here is the book (that) I need.
> *Monsieur Béry, dont le fils est avocat, est maintenant en France.* / Mr. Béry, whose son is a lawyer, is now in France.

ce dont / what, of which, that of which

> *Je ne trouve pas ce dont j'ai besoin.* / I don't find what I need.
> *Ce dont vous parlez est absurde.* / What you are talking about is absurd.

ce que (ce qu') / what, that which

> *Comprenez-vous ce que je vous dis?* / Do you understand what I am telling you?
> *Comprenez-vous ce qu'elle vous dit?* / Do you understand what she is saying to you?
> *Je comprends ce que vous dites et je comprends ce qu'elle dit.* / I understand what you are saying and I understand what she is saying.

ce qui / what, that which

> *Ce qui est vrai est vrai.* / What is true is true.
> *Je ne sais pas ce qui s'est passé.* / I don't know what happened.

Note that *ce qui* is a subject.

lequel (in all its forms) / which

As a relative pronoun, *lequel* (in its various forms) is used as object of a preposition referring to things.

Donnez-moi un autre morceau de papier sur lequel je peux écrire mon adresse. / Give me another piece of paper on which I can write my address.

- *où* / where, in which, on which

    Aimez-vous la salle à manger où nous mangeons? / Do you like the dining room where we eat?
    Je vais ouvrir le tiroir où j'ai mis l'argent. / I am going to open the drawer where I put the money.

- *que* or *qu'* / whom, which, that

    Le garçon que vous voyez là-bas est mon meilleur ami. / The boy whom you see over there is my best friend.
    La composition qu'elle a écrite est excellente. / The composition (that) she wrote is excellent.

- *qui* / who, whom, which, that

    Connais-tu la jeune fille qui parle avec mon frère? / Do you know the girl who is talking with my brother?
    Avez-vous une bicyclette qui marche bien? / Do you have a bicycle that (which) runs well?

§6.1–14 *C'est* + adjective + *à* + infinitive

C'est difficile à faire. / It is difficult to do.

Use this construction when what is being referred to has already been mentioned.

EXAMPLES

Le devoir pour demain est difficile, n'est-ce pas? / The homework for tomorrow is difficult, isn't it?
Oui, c'est difficile à faire. / Yes, it [the homework] is difficult to do.

J'aimerais faire une blouse. / I would like to make a blouse.
C'est facile à faire! Je vais vous montrer. / It's easy to do! I'll show you.

§6.1–15   *Il est* + adjective + *de* + infinitive

Il est impossible de lire ce gros livre en une heure. / It is
   impossible to read this thick book within one hour.

Use this construction when the thing that is impossible,
or difficult, or easy (or any adjective) to do is mentioned in
the same sentence at the same time.

§6.1–16   Neuter Pronoun *le*

The word *le* is the masculine singular definite article. It is
also the masculine singular direct object. *Le* is used as a
neuter pronoun and functions as a direct object referring to
an adjective, a phrase, a clause, or a complete statement. It
is generally not translated into English, except to mean
"it"or "so."

Janine est jolie, mais Henriette ne l'est pas. / Janine is pretty,
   but Henrietta isn't.
*Moi, je crois qu'ils vont gagner le match, et vous? Je le crois
aussi.* / I think they are going to win the game, and you?
   I think so too.

To get a picture of what the word order is when you
have more than one pronoun of any kind in a sentence, see
Word Order of Elements in French Sentences, §11.

§7.

Verbs

§7.1 AGREEMENT

SUBJECT AND VERB
A subject and its corresponding verb form must agree in
person (first, second, or third) and number (singular or plural).

EXAMPLE:
Je vais au cinéma. / I'm going to the movies.

**SUBJECT AND REFLEXIVE PRONOUN OF A
REFLEXIVE VERB**
A subject and reflexive pronoun must agree in person and
number.

EXAMPLE
Je me lave tous les matins. / I wash myself every morning.

SUBJECT AND PAST PARTICIPLE OF AN *ÊTRE* VERB
The past participle of an *être* verb agrees with the subject
in gender and number.

Elle est allée au cinéma. / She went to the movies. OR She has
                                        gone to the movies.
Elles sont allées au cinéma. / They went to the movies. OR
                                        They have gone to the movies.

**PRECEDING REFLEXIVE PRONOUN AND PAST
PARTICIPLE OF A REFLEXIVE VERB**

Elle s'est lavée. / She washed herself.
Elles se sont lavées. / They washed themselves.

However, there is *no* agreement made with the past participle of a reflexive verb if the reflexive pronoun serves as an indirect object pronoun. In the following example, *se* (*s'*) is the indirect object; *les mains* the direct object.

Elle s'est lavé les mains. / She washed her hands.
Elles se sont lavé les mains. / They washed their hands.

Note this:

Elles se sont regardées. / They looked at each other.

Here, the reflexive pronoun *se* serves as the direct object. How do you know? There is no other obvious direct object mentioned, so what they looked at was *se* (each other); of course, you have to look at the subject to see what the gender and number is of the reflexive pronoun *se* in the sentence you are dealing with. The action of the verb is reciprocal.

Remember that the verb *regarder* in French means "to look at" in English; the preposition "at" is not expressed with *à* in French; it is included in the verb—that is why we are dealing with the reflexive pronoun as a direct object here, not an indirect object pronoun.

This same sentence, *Elles se sont regardées,* might also mean: "They looked at themselves." The principle of agreement is still the same. If you mean to say "They looked at each other," in order to avoid two meanings, add *l'une et l'autre.* If more than two persons, add *les unes les autres.*

And note:

Elles se sont parlé au téléphone. / They talked to each other on
the telephone.

Here, the reflexive pronoun *se* is the indirect object
because they spoke to each other; *parler à* is what you a
dealing with here. And remember that no agreement is
made on a past participle with an indirect object. The acti
of the verb is reciprocal.

PAST PARTICIPLE OF AN *AVOIR* VERB WITH A PRECEDING DIRECT OBJECT

EXAMPLES
Je l'ai vue au concert. / I saw her at the concert.

- There is agreement on the past participle *(vue)* because th
  preceding direct object is *la (l')*. Agreement is made in
  gender and number.

  Aimez-vous les fleurs que je vous ai données? / Do you like th
     flowers (that) I gave you?

- There is agreement on the past participle *(données)* of thi
  avoir verb because there is a preceding direct object, *les
  fleurs;* the relative pronoun *que* refers to *les fleurs.* Since
  this direct object noun precedes the verb, the past particip
  must agree in gender and number. A preceding direct
  object, therefore, can be a pronoun or noun.

  Quels films avez-vous vus? / What films did you see?

- There is agreement on the past participle *(vus)* of this avo
  verb because the preceding direct object, *films,* is a mascu
  line plural noun.

  Avez-vous mangé les pâtisseries? / Did you eat the pastries?
  Oui, je les ai mangées. / Yes, I ate them.

In the response to this question, there is agreement on the past participle *(mangées)* of this *avoir* verb because the preceding direct object, *les,* refers to *les pâtisseries,* a feminine plural noun.

J'en ai mangé assez. / I ate enough (of them).

There is no agreement on the past participle *(mangé)* of this *avoir* verb because the preceding direct object is, in this sentence, the pronoun *en.* We do not normally make an agreement with *en,* whether it precedes or follows. This is an exception.

§7.2 PAST PARTICIPLE

REGULAR FORMATION

Infinitive	Type Ending	Drop	Add	Past Participle
donner	-er	-er	é	donné
finir	-ir	-ir	i	fini
vendre	-re	-re	u	vendu

COMMON IRREGULAR PAST PARTICIPLES

Infinitive	Past Participle
apprendre	appris
asseoir	assis
avoir	eu
boire	bu
comprendre	compris
conduire	conduit
connaître	connu
construire	construit
courir	couru

COMMON IRREGULAR PAST PARTICIPLES (cont.)

Infinitive	Past Participle
couvrir	*couvert*
craindre	*craint*
croire	*cru*
devenir	*devenu*
devoir	*dû*
dire	*dit*
écrire	*écrit*
être	*été*
faire	*fait*
falloir	*fallu*
lire	*lu*
mettre	*mis*
mourir	*mort*
naître	*né*
offrir	*offert*
ouvrir	*ouvert*
paraître	*paru*
permettre	*permis*
plaire	*plu*
pleuvoir	*plu*
pouvoir	*pu*
prendre	*pris*
promettre	*promis*
recevoir	*reçu*
revenir	*revenu*
rire	*ri*
savoir	*su*
suivre	*suivi*
taire	*tu*
tenir	*tenu*
valoir	*valu*
venir	*venu*
vivre	*vécu*
voir	*vu*
vouloir	*voulu*

§7.3 TYPES

§7.3–1 Auxiliary Verbs *avoir* and *être*

he auxiliary (helping) verbs *avoir* and *être* are used in any
f the seven simple tenses + the past participle of the main
erb you are using to form any of the compound tenses.
ou must be careful to choose the proper helping verb with
∗e main verb. Some verbs take *avoir* and some take *être*
∗ form the compound tenses.

∗ost French verbs are conjugated with *avoir* to form a
ompound tense.
ll reflexive verbs, such as *se laver,* are conjugated with *être.*

he following is a list of common nonreflexive verbs that
∗re conjugated with *être.*

1. *aller* to go   *Elle est allée au cinéma.*
2. *arriver* to arrive   *Elle est arrivée.*
3. **descendre* to go down, come down   *Elle est
   descendue vite.* / She came down quickly. BUT: **Elle a
   descendu la valise.* / She brought down the suitcase.
4. *devenir* to become   *Elle est devenue folle.*
5. *entrer* to enter, go in, come in   *Elle est entrée.*
6. **monter* to go up, come up   *Elle est montée lentement.* /
   She went up slowly. BUT: **Elle a monté l'escalier.* /
   She went up the stairs.
7. *mourir* to die   *Elle est morte.*
8. *naître* to be born   *Elle est née le premier octobre.*
9. *partir* to leave   *Elle est partie.*
0. **passer* to go by, pass by   *Elle est passée par chez
   moi.* / She came by my house. BUT: **Elle m'a passé le
   sel.* / She passed me the salt. AND: **Elle a passé un
   examen.* / She took an exam.
1. **rentrer* to go in again; to return (home)   *Elle est
   rentrée tôt.* / She returned home early. BUT: **Elle a
   rentré le chat dans la maison.* / She brought (took) the
   cat into the house.
2. *rester* to remain, stay   *Elle est restée chez elle.*

13. *retourner* to return, go back *Elle est retournée.*
14. *revenir* to come back *Elle est revenue.*
15. **sortir* to go out *Elle est sortie hier soir.* / She went out last night. BUT: **Elle a sorti son mouchoir.* / She took out her handkerchief.
16. *tomber* to fall *Elle est tombée.*
17. *venir* to come *Elle est venue.*

---

* Some of these verbs, as noted above, are conjugated with *avoir* if the verb is used in a transitive sense and has a direct object.

§7.3–2 Transitive Verbs

A transitive verb is a verb that takes a direct object. It is transitive because the action passes over and directly affects something or someone in some way.

Je vois mon ami. / I see my friend. →*Je le vois.* / I see him.
Je ferme la fenêtre. / I am closing the window. →*Je la ferme.* / I'm closing it.

When the direct object of the verb is a pronoun, it is usually placed in front of the verb. The only time it is placed after the verb is in the affirmative imperative. To get an idea of the position of direct object pronouns, see Word Order of Elements in French Sentences, §11.

§7.3–3 Intransitive Verbs

An intransitive verb is a verb that does not take a direct object. Such a verb is called intransitive because the action does not pass over and directly affect anyone or anything.

La maîtresse parle. / The teacher is talking.
Elle est partie tôt. / She left early.
Elles sont descendues vite. / They came down quickly.
Nous sommes montées lentement. / We went up slowly.

An intransitive verb takes an indirect object.

La maîtresse parle aux élèves. / The teacher is talking to the
students.

Here the indirect object noun is *élèves* because it is preceded by *aux* / to the.

La maîtresse leur parle. / The teacher is talking to them.

Here the indirect object is the pronoun *leur,* meaning ''to them.''

§7.4 PRESENT PARTICIPLE

Regular Formation

The present participle is regularly formed in the following way: Take the *nous* form of the present indicative tense of the verb you have in mind, drop the first person plural ending *-ons,* and add *-ant.* That ending is equivalent to *-ing* in English.

Infinitive	Present Tense 1st Person Pl.	Drop -ons	add -ant	Present Participle
finir / to finish	*nous finissons*	*finiss*	*ant*	*finissant*
manger / to eat	*nous mangeons*	*mange*	*ant*	*mangeant*
vendre / to sell	*nous vendons*	*vend*	*ant*	*vendant*
faire / to do; make	*nous faisons*	*fais*	*ant*	*faisant*
dire / to say; tell	*nous disons*	*dis*	*ant*	*disant*

Common Irregular Present Participles

Infinitive	Present Participle
avoir to have	*ayant*
être to be	*étant*
savoir to know	*sachant*

Mnemonic tip If you're not sure which is a present participle and which is a past participle in French, associate the n in present with the *n* in the French ending *-ant* of a present participle.

En + Present Participle

The present participle in French is used primarily with the preposition *en,* meaning "on," "upon," "in," "while," "by."

en chantant / while singing
en finissant / upon finishing
en vendant / by selling
en mangeant / upon eating, while eating
en voyageant / by traveling
en ayant / on having
en étant / on being, upon being
en sachant / upon knowing

The present participle is sometimes used as an adjective.

un enfant amusant / an amusing child (boy)
une enfant amusante / an amusing child (girl)

§7.5 VERBS AND PREPOSITIONS

Verb + *à* + Noun or Pronoun

- *assister à quelque chose (à un assemblage, à une réunion, à un spectacle, etc.)* / to attend or be present at (a gathering, a meeting, a theatrical presentation, etc.)

  Allez-vous assister à la conférence du professeur Godard? / Are you going to attend (be present at) Professor Godard's lecture? —*Oui, je vais y assister.* / Yes, I am going to attend it.

- *demander à quelqu'un* / to ask someone

  Demandez à la dame où s'arrête l'autobus. / Ask the lady where the bus stops.

- *désobéir à quelqu'un* / to disobey someone

  Ce chien ne désobéit jamais à son maître. / This dog never disobeys his master.
  Il ne lui désobéit jamais. / He never disobeys him.

- *être à quelqu'un* / to belong to someone

  Ce livre est à Victor. / This book belongs to Victor.

- *faire attention à quelqu'un ou à quelque chose* / to pay attention to someone or to something

  Faites attention au professeur. / Pay attention to the professor.

- *s'intéresser à quelqu'un ou à quelque chose* / to be interested in someone or something

  Je m'intéresse aux sports. / I am interested in sports.

- *jouer à* / to play (a game or sport)

  Il aime bien jouer à la balle. / He likes to play ball.
  Elle aime bien jouer au tennis. / She likes to play tennis.

- *obéir à quelqu'un* / to obey someone

  Une personne honorable obéit à ses parents. / An honorable person obeys his (her) parents.

• *participer à quelque chose* / to participate in something

> *Je participe aux sports.* / I participate in sports.

• *penser à quelqu'un ou à quelque chose* / to think of (about) someone or something

> *Je pense à mes amis.* / I am thinking of my friends.
> *Je pense à eux.* / I am thinking of them.
> *Je pense à mon travail.* / I am thinking about my work.
> *J'y pense.* / I am thinking about it.

• *répondre à quelqu'un ou à quelque chose* / to answer someone or something

> *J'ai répondu au professeur.* / I answered the teacher.
> *Je lui ai répondu.* / I answered him.
> *J'ai répondu à la lettre.* / I answered the letter.
> *J'y ai répondu.* / I answered it.

• *ressembler à quelqu'un* / to resemble someone

> *Il ressemble beaucoup à sa mère.* / He resembles his mother a lot.

• *réussir à quelque chose* / to succeed in something
réussir à un examen / to pass an examination

> *Il a réussi à l'examen.* / He passed the exam.

• *téléphoner à quelqu'un* / to telephone someone

> *Marie a téléphoné à Paul.* / Marie telephoned Paul.
> *Elle lui a téléphoné.* / She telephoned him.

Verb + à + Infinitive

• *aider à* / to help

> *Roger aide son petit frère à faire son devoir de mathématiques.*
> Roger is helping his little brother to do his math homework.

• *s'amuser à* / to amuse oneself, enjoy, have fun

> *Il y a des élèves qui s'amusent à mettre le professeur en colère.* / There are pupils who enjoy making the teacher angry.

• *apprendre à* / to learn

> *J'apprends à lire.* / I am learning to read.

• *s'attendre à* / to expect

> *Je m'attendais à trouver une salle de classe vide.* / I was expecting to find an empty classroom.

• *avoir à* / to have to, to be obliged to (do something)

> *J'ai mes devoirs à faire ce soir.* / I have to do my homework tonight.

• *commencer à* / to begin

> *Il commence à pleuvoir.* / It is beginning to rain.

• *continuer à* / to continue

> *Je continue à étudier le français.* / I am continuing to study French.

• *décider quelqu'un à* / to persuade someone

> *J'ai décidé mon père à me prêter quelques francs.* / I persuaded my father to lend me a few francs.

• *se décider à* / to make up one's mind

> *Il s'est décidé à l'épouser.* / He made up his mind to marry her.

• *demander à* / to ask, request

> *Elle demande à parler.* / She asks to speak.

• *encourager à* / to encourage

> *Je l'ai encouragé à suivre un cours de français.* / I encouraged him to take a course in French.

• *enseigner à* / to teach

> *Je vous enseigne à lire en français.* / I am teaching you to read in French.

- *s'habituer à* / to get used (to)

   Je m'habitue à parler français couramment. / I am getting used to speaking French fluently.

- *hésiter à* / to hesitate

   J'hésite à répondre à sa lettre. / I hesitate to reply to her (his) letter.

- *inviter à* / to invite

   Monsieur et Madame Boivin ont invité les Béry à dîner chez eux. / Mr. and Mrs. Boivin invited the Bérys to have dinner at their house.

- *se mettre à* / to begin

   L'enfant se met à rire. / The child is beginning to laugh.

- *parvenir à* / to succeed

   Elle est parvenue à être docteur. / She succeeded in becoming a doctor.

- *se plaire à* / to take pleasure in

   Il se plaît à taquiner ses amis. / He takes pleasure in teasing his friends.

- *recommencer à* / to begin again

   Il recommence à pleuvoir. / It is beginning to rain again.

- *réussir à* / to succeed in

   Henri a réussi à me convaincre. / Henry succeeded in convincing me.

- *songer à* / to dream; to think

   Elle songe à trouver un millionnaire. / She is dreaming of finding a millionaire.

•*tenir à* / to insist, be anxious

Je tiens absolument à voir mon enfant immédiatement. / I am very anxious to see my child immediately.

Verb + *de* + Noun

•*s'agir de* / to be a question of, a matter of

Il s'agit de l'amour. / It is a matter of love.

•*s'approcher de* / to approach

La dame s'approche de la porte et elle l'ouvre. / The lady approaches the door and opens it.

•*changer de* / to change

Je dois changer de train à Paris. / I have to change trains in Paris.

•*se douter de* / to suspect

Je me doute de ses opinions. / I suspect his (her) opinions.

•*féliciter de* / to congratulate on

Je vous félicite de vos progrès. / I congratulate you on your progress.

•*jouer de* / to play (a musical instrument)

Je sais jouer du piano. / I know how to play the piano.

•*manquer de* / to lack

Cette personne manque de politesse. / This person lacks courtesy.

•*se méfier de* / to distrust, to mistrust, to beware of

Je me méfie des personnes que je ne connais pas. / I distrust persons whom I do not know.

•*se moquer de* / to make fun of

Les enfants aiment se moquer d'un singe. / Children like to make fun of a monkey.

- *s'occuper de* / to be busy with

  > *Madame Boulanger s'occupe de son mari infirme.* / Mrs. Boulanger is busy with her disabled husband.
  > *Je m'occupe de mes affaires.* / I mind my own business.
  > *Occupez-vous de vos affaires!* / Mind your own business!

- *partir de* / to leave

  > *Il est parti de la maison à huit heures.* / He left the house at eight o'clock.

- *se plaindre de* / to complain about

  > *Il se plaint toujours de son travail.* / He always complains about his work.

- *remercier de* / to thank

  > *Je vous remercie de votre bonté.* / I thank you for your kindness

  (Use *remercier de* + an abstract noun or infinitive; *remercier pour* + a concrete object; e.g., *Je vous remercie pour le cadeau.* / I thank you for the present.)

- *se rendre compte de* / to realize, to be aware of

  > *Je me rends compte de la condition de cette personne.* / I am aware of the condition of this person.

- *se servir de* / to employ, use, make use of

  > *Je me sers d'un stylo quand j'écris une lettre.* / I use a pen when I write a letter.

- *se souvenir de* / to remember

  > *Oui, je me souviens de Gervaise.* / Yes, I remember Gervaise.
  > *Je me souviens de lui.* / I remember him.
  > *Je me souviens d'elle.* / I remember her.
  > *Je me souviens de l'été passé.* / I remember last summer.
  > *Je m'en souviens.* / I remember it.

• *tenir de* / to take after (to resemble)

> *Julie tient de sa mère.* / Julie takes after her mother.

Verb + *de* + Infinitive

• *s'agir de* / to be a question of, a matter of

> *Il s'agit de faire les devoirs tous les jours.* / It is a matter of doing the homework every day.

• *avoir peur de* / to be afraid of

> *Le petit garçon a peur de traverser la rue seul.* / The little boy is afraid of crossing the street alone.

• *cesser de* / to stop, cease

> *Il a cessé de pleuvoir.* / It has stopped raining.

• *craindre de* / to be afraid of, fear

> *La petite fille craint de traverser la rue seule.* / The little girl is afraid of crossing the street alone.

• *décider de* / to decide

> *J'ai décidé de partir tout de suite.* / I decided to leave immediately.

• *demander de* / to ask, request

> *Je vous demande de parler.* / I am asking you to speak.

> [Note that here the subjects are different: *I* am asking *you* to speak; but when the subjects are the same, use *demander à*: *Elle demande à parler.* / She is asking to speak.]

• *se dépêcher de* / to hurry

> *Je me suis dépêché de venir chez vous pour vous dire quelque chose.* / I hurried to come to your place in order to tell you something.

- *empêcher de* / to keep from, prevent

    Je vous empêche de sortir. / I prevent you from going out.

- *essayer de* / to try

    J'essaye d'ouvrir la porte mais je ne peux pas. / I'm trying to
    open the door but I can't.

- *féliciter de* / to congratulate

    On m'a félicité d'avoir gagné le prix. / I was congratulated on
    having won the prize.

- *finir de* / to finish

    J'ai fini de travailler sur cette composition. / I have finished
    working on this composition.

- *se hâter de* / to hurry

    Je me hâte de venir chez toi. / I am hurrying to come to your
    house.

- *offrir de* / to offer

    J'ai offert d'écrire une lettre pour elle. / I offered to write a
    letter for her.

- *oublier de* / to forget

    J'ai oublié de vous donner la monnaie. / I forgot to give you the
    change.

- *persuader de* / to persuade

    J'ai persuadé mon père de me prêter quelques francs. / I
    persuaded my father to lend me a few francs.

- *prendre garde de* / to take care not to

    Prenez garde de tomber. / Be careful not to fall.

prier de/ to beg

> *Je vous prie d'arrêter./* I beg you to stop.

promettre de/ to promise

> *J'ai promis de venir chez toi à huit heures./* I promised to come to your place at eight o'clock.

refuser de/ to refuse

> *Je refuse de le croire./* I refuse to believe it.

regretter de/ to regret, be sorry

> *Je regrette d'être obligé de vous dire cela./* I am sorry to be obliged to tell you that.

● *remercier de/* to thank

> *Je vous remercie d'être venu si vite./* I thank you for coming (having come) so quickly. (Use *remercier de* + infinitive or + abstract noun. Use *remercier pour* + concrete object.)

● *se souvenir de/* to remember

> *Tu vois? Je me suis souvenu de venir chez toi./* You see? I remembered to come to your house.

● *tâcher de/* to try

> *Tâche de finir tes devoirs avant de sortir./* Try to finish your homework before going out.

● *venir de/* to have just (done something)

> *Je viens de manger./* I have just eaten. (I just ate.)

Verb + *à* + Noun + *de* + Infinitive

The model to follow is: *J'ai conseillé à Robert de suivre un cours de français.* / I advised Robert to take a course in French.

- *conseiller à* / to advise

    J'ai conseillé à Jeanne de se marier. / I advised Joan to get married.

- *défendre à* / to forbid

    Mon père défend à mon frère de fumer. / My father forbids my brother to smoke.

- *demander à* / to ask, request

    J'ai demandé à Marie de venir. / I asked Mary to come.

- *dire à* / to say, to tell

    J'ai dit à Charles de venir. / I told Charles to come.

- *interdire à* / to forbid

    Mon père interdit à mon frère de fumer. / My father forbids my brother to smoke.

- *permettre à* / to permit

    J'ai permis à l'étudiant de partir quelques minutes avant la fin de la classe. / I permitted the student to leave a few minutes before the end of class.

- *promettre à* / to promise

    J'ai promis à mon ami d'arriver à l'heure. / I promised my friend to arrive on time.

- *téléphoner à* / to telephone

    J'ai téléphoné à Marcel de venir me voir. / I phoned Marcel to come to see me.

Verb + Other Prepositions

- *commencer par* + infinitive / to begin by + present participle

    La présidente a commencé par discuter des problèmes de la société. / The president began by discussing problems in society.

* *s'entendre avec quelqu'un* / to get along with someone

   Jean s'entend avec Christophe. / John gets along with Christopher.

entrer dans + noun/ to enter, go in

   Elle est entrée dans le restaurant./ She went into the restaurant.

insister pour + infinitive/ to insist on, upon

   J'insiste pour obtenir tous mes droits./ I insist on obtaining all my rights.

se marier avec quelqu'un/ to marry someone

   Elle va se marier avec lui./ She is going to marry him.

se mettre en colère/ to become angry, upset

   Monsieur Leduc se met en colère facilement./ Mr. Leduc gets angry easily.

se mettre en route/ to start out, set out

   Ils se sont mis en route dès l'aube./ They started out at dawn.

remercier pour + a concrete noun/ to thank for

   Je vous remercie pour le joli cadeau./ I thank you for the pretty present. (Remember to use *remercier de* + an abstract noun or + infinitive: *Je vous remercie de votre bonté.*/ I thank you for your kindness. *Je vous remercie d'être venue si vite.*/ I thank you for coming so quickly.)

Verb + no preposition + Infinitive

The following verbs take *no* preposition and are followed directly by the infinitive.

adorer/ to adore, love

   Madame Morin adore mettre tous ses bijoux avant de sortir. Mrs. Morin loves to put on all her jewelry before going out.

- *aimer*/ to like

    J'aime lire./ I like to read.

- *aimer mieux*/ to prefer

    J'aime mieux rester ici./ I prefer to stay here.

- *aller*/ to go

    Je vais faire mes devoirs./ I am going to do my homework.

- *compter*/ to intend

    Je compte aller en France l'été prochain./ I intend to go to France next summer.

- *croire*/ to believe

    Il croit être innocent./ He believes he is innocent.

- *désirer*/ to desire, wish

    Je désire prendre une tasse de café./ I wish to have a cup of coffee.

- *devoir*/ to have to, ought to

    Je dois faire mes devoirs avant de sortir./ I have to do my homework before going out.

- *écouter*/ to listen to

    J'écoute chanter les enfants./ I am listening to the children singing.

- *entendre*/ to hear

    J'entends chanter les enfants./ I hear the children singing.

- *espérer*/ to hope

    J'espère aller en France./ I hope to go to France.

- *faire*/ to cause; to make; to have something done by someone

    Le professeur fait travailler les élèves dans la salle de classe. The teacher has the pupils work in the classroom.

- *falloir*/ to be necessary

    Il faut être honnête./ One must be honest.

- *laisser*/ to let, allow

    Je vous laisse partir./ I am letting you go.

- *paraître*/ to appear, seem

    Elle paraît être capable./ She appears to be capable.

- *penser*/ to think, plan, intend

    Je pense aller à Paris./ I intend to go to Paris.

- *pouvoir*/ to be able, can

    Je peux marcher mieux maintenant./ I can walk better now.

- *préférer*/ to prefer

    Je préfère manger maintenant./ I prefer to eat now.

- *regarder*/ to look at

    Je regarde voler les oiseaux./ I am looking at the birds flying.

- *savoir* / to know, know how

    Je sais nager. / I know how to swim.

- *valoir mieux* / to be better

    Il vaut mieux être honnête. / It is better to be honest.

- *vouloir* / to want

    Je veux venir chez vous. / I want to come to your house.

Verbs That Do Not Require a Preposition

- *attendre* / to wait for

    J'attends l'autobus depuis vingt minutes. / I have been waiting for the bus for twenty minutes.

- *chercher* / to look for

    Je cherche mon livre. / I'm looking for my book.

- *demander* / to ask for

    Je demande une réponse. / I am asking for a reply.

- *écouter* / to listen to

    J'écoute la musique. / I am listening to the music.
    J'écoute le professeur. / I am listening to the teacher.

- *envoyer chercher* / to send for

    J'ai envoyé chercher le docteur. / I sent for the doctor.

- *essayer* / to try on

    Elle a essayé une jolie robe. / She tried on a pretty dress.

- *mettre* / to put on

    Elle a mis la robe rouge. / She put on the red dress.

- *payer* / to pay for

    J'ai payé le dîner. / I paid for the dinner.

- *pleurer* / to cry about, cry over

    Elle pleure la perte de son petit chien. / She is crying over the loss of her little dog.

- *regarder* / to look at

    Je regarde le ciel. / I am looking at the sky.

§7.6 COMPLETE CONJUGATION OF AN *AVOIR* VERB

Present participle: *parlant* / talking, speaking; Past participle: *parlé* / talked, spoken; Infinitive: *parler* / to talk, to speak

| Present indicative | *je parle, tu parles, il (elle, on) parle; nous parlons, vous parlez, ils (elles) parlent* |

I talk, you talk, he (she, it, one) talks; we talk, you talk, they talk

OR

I do talk, etc.

OR

I am talking, etc.

Imperfect indicative	*je parlais, tu parlais, il (elle, on) parlait; nous parlions, vous parliez, ils (elles) parlaient*

I was talking, you were talking, he (she, it, one) was talking; we were talking, you were talking, they were talking

OR

I used to talk, etc.

OR

I talked, etc.

Past definite	*je parlai, tu parlas, il (elle, on) parla; nous parlâmes, vous parlâtes, ils (elles) parlèrent*

I talked, you talked, he (she, it, one) talked; we talked, you talked, they talked

OR

I did talk, etc.

Future	*je parlerai, tu parleras, il (elle, on) parlera; nous parlerons, vous parlerez, ils (elles) parleront*

I shall talk, you will talk, he (she, it, one) will talk; we shall talk, you will talk, they will talk

Conditional present	*je parlerais, tu parlerais, il (elle, on) parlerait; nous parlerions, vous parleriez, ils (elles) parleraient*

I would talk, you would talk, he (she, it, one) would talk; we would talk, you would talk, they would talk

Present subjunctive

que je parle, que tu parles, qu'il (qu'elle, qu'on) parle; que nous parlions, que vous parliez, qu'ils (qu'elles) parlent

that I may talk, that you may talk, that he (she, it, one) may talk; that we may talk, that you may talk, that they may talk

Imperfect subjunctive

que je parlasse, que tu parlasses, qu'il (qu'elle, qu'on) parlât; que nous parlassions, que vous parlassiez, qu'ils (qu'elles) parlassent

that I might talk, that you might talk, that he (she, it, one) might talk; that we might talk, that you might talk, that they might talk

Past indefinite

j'ai parlé, tu as parlé, il (elle, on) a parlé; nous avons parlé, vous avez parlé, ils (elles) ont parlé

I talked, you talked, he (she, it, one) talked; we talked, you talked, they talked

OR

I have talked, you have talked, he (she, it, one) has talked; we have talked, you have talked, they have talked

OR

I did talk, you did talk, he (she, it, one) did talk; we did talk, you did talk, they did talk

Pluperfect indicative

j'avais parlé, tu avais parlé, il (elle, on) avait parlé; nous avions parlé, vous aviez parlé, ils (elles) avaient parlé

I had talked, you had talked, he (she, it, one) had talked; we had talked, you had talked, they had talked

**Past
Interior**

j'eus parlé, tu eus parlé, il (elle, on) eut parlé; nous eûmes parlé, vous eûtes parlé, ils (elles) eurent parlé

I had talked, you had talked, he (she, it, one) had talked; we had talked, you had talked, they had talked

**Future
Perfect**

j'aurai parlé, tu auras parlé, il (elle, on) aura parlé; nous aurons parlé, vous aurez parlé, ils (elles) auront parlé

I shall have talked, you will have talked, he (she, it, one) will have talked; we shall have talked, you will have talked, they will have talked

**Conditional
Perfect**

j'aurais parlé, tu aurais parlé, il (elle, on) aurait parlé; nous aurions parlé, vous auriez parlé, ils (elles) auraient parlé

I would have talked, you would have talked, he (she, it, one) would have talked; we would have talked, you would have talked, they would have talked

**Past
Subjunctive**

que j'aie parlé, que tu aies parlé, qu'il (qu'elle, qu'on) ait parlé; que nous ayons parlé, que vous ayez parlé, qu'ils (qu'elles) aient parlé

that I may have talked, that you may have talked, that he (she, it, one) may have talked; that we may have talked, that you may have talked, that they may have talked

Pluperfect *que j'eusse parlé, que tu eusses parlé, qu'il*
subjunctive *(qu'elle, qu'on) eût parlé; que nous eussions
parlé, que vous eussiez parlé, qu'ils (qu'elles)
eussent parlé*

> that I might have talked, that you might have
> talked, that he (she, it, one) might have talked,
> that we might have talked, that you might
> have talked, that they might have talked

Imperative *parle, parlons, parlez*

> talk, let's talk, talk

§7.7 COMPLETE CONJUGATION OF AN *ÊTRE* VERB

Present participle: *venant*/ coming; Past participle; *venu*/
come; Infinitive: *venir*/ to come

Present *je viens, tu viens, il (elle, on) vient; nous*
indicative *venons, vous venez, ils (elles) viennent*

> I come, you come, he (she, it, one) comes; we
> come, you come, they come
>
> OR
>
> I do come, etc.
>
> OR
>
> I am coming, etc.

Imperfect *je venais, tu venais, il (elle, on) venait; nous*
indicative *venions, vous veniez, ils (elles) venaient*

> I was coming, you were coming, he (she, it,
> one) was coming; we were coming, you were

coming, they were coming

OR

I used to come, etc.

OR

I came, etc.

Past
definite

*je vins, tu vins, il (elle, on) vint; nous vînmes,
vous vîntes, ils (elles) vinrent*

I came, you came, he (she, it, one) came; we
came, you came, they came

OR

I did come, etc.

Future

*je viendrai, tu viendras, il (elle, on) viendra;
nous viendrons, vous viendrez, ils (elles)
viendront*

I shall come, you will come, he (she, it, one)
will come; we shall come, you will come, they
will come

Conditional
present

*je viendrais, tu viendrais, il (elle, on) viendrait;
nous viendrions, vous viendriez, ils (elles)
viendraient*

I would come, you would come, he (she, it,
one) would come; we would come, you would
come, they would come

Present
subjunctive

*que je vienne, que tu viennes, qu'il (qu'elle,
qu'on) vienne; que nous venions, que vous
veniez, qu'ils (qu'elles) viennent*

that I may come, that you may come, that he
(she, it, one) may come; that we may come,
that you may come, that they may come

Imperfect subjunctive	*que je vinsse, que tu vinsses, qu'il (qu'elle, qu'on) vînt; que nous vinssions, que vous vinssiez, qu'ils (qu'elles) vinssent*

that I might come, that you might come, that he (she, it, one) might come; that we might come, that you might come; that they might come

Past indefinite	*je suis venu(e), tu es venu(e), il (on) est venu, elle est venue; nous sommes venu(e)s, vous êtes venu(e)(s), ils sont venus, elles sont venues*

I came, you came, he (she, it, one) came; we came, you came, they came

OR

I have come, etc.

OR

I did come, etc.

Pluperfect indicative	*j'étais venu(e), tu étais venu(e), il, on était venu, elle était venue; nous étions venu(e)s, vous étiez venu(e)(s), ils étaient venus, elles étaient venues*

I had come, you had come, he (she, it, one) had come; we had come, you had come, they had come

Past anterior	*je fus venu(e), tu fus venu(e), il (on) fut venu, elle fut venue; nous fûmes venu(e)s, vous fûtes venu(e)(s), ils furent venus, elles furent venues*

I had come, you had come, he (she, it, one) had come; we had come, you had come, they had come

Future
perfect

*je serai venu(e), tu seras venu(e), il (on) sera
venu, elle sera venue; nous serons venu(e)s,
vous serez venu(e)(s), ils seront venus, elles
seront venues*

I shall have come, you will have come, he
(she, it, one) will have come; we shall have
come, you will have come, they will have come

Conditional
perfect

*je serais venu(e), tu serais venu(e), il (on)
serait venu, elle serait venue; nous serions
venu(e)s, vous seriez venu(e)(s), ils seraient
venus, elles seraient venues*

I would have come, you would have come, he
(she, it, one) would have come; we would
have come, you would have come, they would
have come

Past
subjunctive

*que je sois venu(e), que tu sois venu(e), qu'il
(on) soit venu, qu'elle soit venue; que nous
soyons venu(e)s, que vous soyez venu(e)(s),
qu'ils soient venus, qu'elles soient venues*

that I may have come, that you may have
come, that he (she, it, one) may have come;
that we may have come, that you may have
come, that they may have come

Pluperfect
subjunctive

*que je fusse venu(e), que tu fusses venu(e),
qu'il (qu'on) fût venu, qu'elle fût venue; que
nous fussions venu(e)s, que vous fussiez
venu(e)(s), qu'ils fussent venus, qu'elles fussent venues*

that I might have come, that you might have
come, that he (she, it, one) might have come;

that we might have come, that you might ha
come, that they might have come

Imperative   *viens, venons, venez*

come, let's come, come

§7.8   TENSES AND MOODS

§7.8–1   Present Indicative Tense

The *present indicative* is the most frequently used tense i
French and English. It indicates:

• An action or a state of being at the present time.

Je vais à l'école maintenant./ I am going to school now.
Je pense; donc, je suis./ I think; therefore, I am.

• Habitual action.

Je vais à la bibliothèque tous les jours./ I go to the library eve
day.

• A general truth, something that is permanently true.

Deux et deux font quatre./ Two and two are four.
Voir c'est croire./ Seeing is believing.

• Vividness when talking or writing about past events.

*Marie-Antoinette est condamnée à mort. Elle monte dans la
charrette qui est en route pour la guillotine./* Marie-Antoinette
condemned to die. She gets into the cart and is on her way
to the guillotine.

• A near future.

Il arrive demain./ He arrives tomorrow.

An action or state of being that occurred in the past and continues up to the present. In English, this tense is the present perfect, which is formed with the present tense of "to have" plus the past participle of the verb you are using.

Je suis ici depuis dix minutes./ I have been here for ten minutes. (I am still here at present.)

This tense is regularly formed as follows:

Drop the *-er* ending of an infinitive like *parler*, and add *-e, -es, -e; -ons, -ez, -ent.*

You then get:
je parle, tu parles, il (elle, on) parle; nous parlons, vous parlez, ils (elles) parlent

Drop the *-ir* ending of an infinitive like *finir*, and add *-is, -is, -it; -issons, -issez, -issent.*

You then get:
je finis, tu finis, il (elle, on) finit; nous finissons, vous finissez, ils (ells) finissent

Drop the *-re* ending of an infinitive like *vendre*, and add *-s, -s, —; -ons, -ez, -ent.*

You then get:
je vends, tu vends, il (elle, on) vend; nous vendons, vous vendez, ils (elles) vendent

For the present tense of *avoir* and *être*, see §7.19.

§7.8–2 Imperfect Indicative Tense

The *imperfect indicative* is a past tense. It is used to indicate:

An action that was going on in the past at the same time as another action.

Il lisait pendant que j'écrivais. / He was reading while I was writing.

- An action that was going on in the past when another action occurred.

  Il lisait quand je suis entré. / He was reading when I came in.

- An action that was performed habitually in the past.

  Nous allions à la plage tous les jours. / We used to go to the beach every day.

- A description of a mental or physical condition in the past.

  (mental) *Il était triste quand je l'ai vu.* / He was sad when I saw him.
  (physical) *Quand ma mère était jeune, elle était belle.* / When my mother was young, she was beautiful.

- An action or state of being that occurred in the past and lasted for a certain length of time prior to another past action

  J'attendais l'autobus depuis dix minutes quand il est arrivé. / I had been waiting for the bus for ten minutes when it arrived.

This tense is regularly formed as follows:

For -er, -ir, and -re verbs, take the "*nous*" form in the present indicative tense of the verb you have in mind, drop the first person plural ending (*-ons*), and add the endings *-ais, -ais, -ait; -ions, -iez, -aient.*

| Mnemonic tip | The vowel *i* is in each of the six endings and *i* is the first letter of the *imperfect* tense

For the imperfect indicative of *avoir* and *être*, see §7.19.

§7.8–3 Past Simple Tense

This past tense expresses an action that took place at some definite time. It is not ordinarily used in conversation

rench or in informal writing. It is a literary tense — used in
ormal writing, such as history and literature.

The past simple tense is regularly formed as follows:
For all *-er* verbs, drop the *-er* of the infinitive and add *-ai,
as, -a; -âmes, -âtes, -èrent.*

For regular *-ir* and *-re* verbs, drop the ending of the
nfinitive and add the endings *-is, -is, -it; -îmes, -îtes, -irent.*

Il alla en Afrique./ He went to Africa.
Il voyagea en Amérique./ He traveled to America.
Elle fut heureuse./ She was happy.
Elle eut un grand bonheur./ She had great happiness.

For the past definite of *avoir* and *être,* see §7.19.

§7.8–4 Future Tense

n French and English the *future* tense is used to express
an action or a state of being which will take place at some
ime in the future.

J'irai en France l'été prochain./ I will go to France next summer.
J'y penserai./ I will think about it.
Je partirai dès qu'il arrivera./ I will leave as soon as he arrives.
Je te dirai tout quand tu seras ici./ I will tell you all when you
    are here.

If the action of the verb you are using is not past or
present and if future time is implied, the future tense is used
vhen the clause begins with the following conjunctions:
aussitôt que/ as soon as, *dès que*/ as soon as, *quand*/
vhen, *lorsque*/ when, and *tant que*/ as long as.

This tense is regularly formed as follows:
Add the following endings to the whole infinitive: *-ai, -as,
a, -ons, -ez, -ont.* For *-re* verbs you must drop the *e* in *-re*
before you add the future endings.

For the future of *avoir* and *être,* see §7.19.

§7.8–5 Conditional Present Tense

The conditional mood is used in French and English to express:

- An action that you would do if something else were possib█

    Je ferais le travail si j'en avais le temps. / I would do the wor█
    I had the time.

- A conditional desire.

    J'aimerais du thé. / I would like some tea.
    Je voudrais du café. / I would like some coffee.

- An obligation or duty.

    Je devrais étudier pour l'examen. / I should study for the
    examination.

The conditional has two tenses, the present and the past

The present conditional is regularly formed as follows:
    Add the following endings to the whole infinitive: *-ais*,
-ais, -ait; -ions, -iez, -aient. For *-re* verbs you must drop t█
e in *-re* before you add the conditional endings. Note that
these endings are the same ones you use to form regular
the imperfect indicative. For the conditional of *avoir* and
être, see §7.19.

§7.8–6 Present Subjunctive Tense

The subjunctive mood is used in French much more than █
English. It is used in the following ways:

- After a verb that expresses some kind of insistence,
preference, or suggestion.

    Nous insistons que vous soyez ici à l'heure. / We insist that y█
    be here on time.

Je préfère qu'il fasse le travail maintenant. / I prefer that he do the work now.
Le juge exige qu'il soit puni. / The judge demands that he be punished.

After a verb that expresses doubt, fear, joy, sorrow, or some other emotion.

Sylvie doute qu'il vienne. / Sylvia doubts that he is coming.
Je suis heureux qu'il vienne. / I'm happy that he is coming.
Je regrette qu'il soit malade. / I'm sorry that he is sick.

After certain conjunctions.

Elle partira à moins qu'il ne vienne. / She will leave unless he comes.
Je resterai jusqu'à ce qu'il vienne. / I will stay until he comes.
Quoiqu'elle soit belle, il ne l'aime pas. / Although she is beautiful, he does not love her.
Le professeur l'explique pour qu'elle comprenne. / The teacher is explaining it so that she may understand.

After certain impersonal expressions that show a need, a doubt, a possibility or an impossibility.

Il est urgent qu'il vienne. / It is urgent that he come.
Il vaut mieux qu'il vienne. / It is better that he come.
Il est possible qu'il vienne. / It is possible that he will come.
Il est douteux qu'il vienne. / It is doubtful that he will come.

The present subjunctive is regularly formed by dropping the *-ant* ending of the present participle of the verb you are using and adding the endings *-e, -es, -e; -ions, -iez, -ent.*

For the present subjunctive of *avoir* and *être*, see §7.19. See also Subjunctive, §7.15.

§7.8–7 Imperfect Subjunctive Tense

The *imperfect subjunctive* is used in the same ways as the present subjunctive, that is, after certain verbs, conjunctions, and impersonal expressions. The main difference between these two is the time of the action. If present, use the present subjunctive. If the action is related to the past, the imperfect subjunctive is used, provided that the action was not completed.

Je voulais qu'il vînt. / I wanted him to come. (action not completed; he did not come while I wanted him to come)

Note: The subjunctive of *venir* is used because *vouloir* requires the subjunctive *after* it. In conversational French and informal writing, the imperfect subjunctive is avoided. Use, instead, the present subjunctive.

Je voulais qu'il vienne. / I wanted him to come.
Je le lui expliquais pour qu'elle le comprît. / I was explaining it to her so that she might understand it. (action not completed; the understanding was not completed at the time of the explaining)

Note: The subjunctive of *comprendre* is used because the conjunction *pour que* requires the subjunctive *after* it Again, avoid using the imperfect subjunctive in conversation and informal writing. Use, instead, the present subjunctive: *Je le lui expliquais pour qu'elle le comprenne*

The imperfect subjunctive is regularly formed by dropping the endings of the *passé simple* of the verb you are using and adding the following endings:

-*er* verbs: -*asse*, -*asses*, -*ât*; -*assions*, -*assiez*, -*assent*
-*ir* verbs: -*isse*, -*isses*, -*ît*; -*issions*, -*issiez*, -*issent*
-*re* verbs: -*usse*, -*usses*, -*ût*; -*ussions*, -*ussiez*, -*ussent*

For the imperfect subjunctive of *avoir* and *être*, see §7.19. See also Subjunctive, §7.15.

7.8–8 Past Indefinite Tense

This past tense expresses an action that took place at no definite time. It is used in conversational French, correspondence, and other informal writing. The past indefinite is used more and more in literature these days and is taking the place of the past definite. It is a compound tense because it is formed with the present indicative of *avoir* or *être* (depending on which of these two auxiliaries is required to form a compound tense) plus the past participle. See 7.3 for the distinction made between verbs conjugated with *avoir* or *être*. This is the *passé composé*.

Il est allé à l'école. / He went to school; He did go to school; He has gone to school.

J'ai mangé dans ce restaurant de nombreuses fois. / I have eaten in this restaurant many times.

J'ai parlé au garçon. / I spoke to the boy; I have spoken to the boy; I did speak to the boy.

7.8–9 Pluperfect Tense

In French and English this tense (also called the *past perfect*) is used to express an action that happened in the past before another past action. Since it is used in relation to another past action, the other past action is expressed in either the past indefinite or the imperfect indicative in French. The pluperfect is used in formal writing and literature as well as in conversational French and informal writing. It is a compound tense because it is formed with the imperfect indicative of *avoir* or *être* (depending on which of these two auxiliaries is required to form a compound tense) plus the past participle. See §7.3 for the distinction made between verbs conjugated with *avoir* or *être*.

Je me suis rappelé que j'avais oublié de le lui dire. / I remembered that I had forgotten to tell him.

Note: It would be incorrect to say: I remembered that I forgot to tell him. The point here is that first I forgot; the I remembered. Both actions are in the past. The action that occurred in the past *before* the other past action is in the pluperfect. And in this example it is "I had forgotten" (*j'avais oublié*).

J'avais étudié la leçon que le professeur a expliquée. / I had studied the lesson that the teacher explained.

Note: First I studied the lesson; then the teacher explained it. Both actions are in the past. The action that occurred in the past before the other past action is in the pluperfect. And in this example it is "I had studied" (*j'avais étudié*).

J'étais fatigué ce matin parce que je n'avais pas dormi. / I was tired this morning because I had not slept.

§7.8–10 Past Anterior Tense

This tense is similar to the pluperfect indicative. The main difference is that in French it is a literary tense; that is, it is used in formal writing such as history and literature. More and more French writers today use the pluperfect indicative instead of the past anterior. The past anterior is a compound tense and is formed with the *passé simple* of *avoir* o *être* (depending on which of these two auxiliaries is required to form a compound tense) plus the past participle. It is ordinarily introduced by conjunctions of time: *après que, aussitôt que, dès que, lorsque, quand.*

Quand il eut tout mangé, il partit. / When he had eaten everything, he left.

§7.8–11 Future Perfect Tense

In French and English this tense (also called the *future anterior*) is used to express an action that will happen in the future *before* another future action. Since it is used in relation to another future action, the other future action is expressed in the simple future in French. It is used in conversation and informal writing as well as in formal writing and in literature. It is a compound tense because it is formed with the future of *avoir* or *être* (depending on which of these two auxiliaries is required to form a compound tense) plus the past participle of the verb you are using. In English, it is formed by using "will have" plus the past participle of the verb you are using.

Elle arrivera demain et j'aurai fini le travail. / She will arrive tomorrow and I will have finished the work.

Note: First I will finish the work; then she will arrive. The action that will occur in the future *before* the other future action is in the future anterior.

Quand elle arrivera demain, j'aurai fini le travail. / When she arrives tomorrow, I will have finished the work.

Note: The idea of future time here is the same as in the preceding example. In English, the present tense is used ("When she arrives . . .") to express a near future. In French, the future is used *(Quand elle arrivera . . .)* because *quand* precedes and the action will take place in the future.

§7.8–12 Conditional Perfect Tense

This is used in French and English to express an action that you would have done if something else had been possible; that is, you would have done something on condition that something else had been possible. It is a compound tense because it is formed with the conditional of *avoir* or *être* plus the past participle of the verb you are using. In English, it is formed by using "would have" plus the past participle.

J'aurais fait le travail si j'avais étudié.   / I would have done the
    work if I had studied.
J'aurais fait le travail si j'en avais eu le temps.   / I would have
    done the work if I had had the time.

§7.8–13   Past Subjunctive Tense

This tense is used to express an action that took place in
the past in relation to the present. It is like the past indefinite, except that the auxiliary verb (*avoir* or *être*) is in the
present subjunctive. The subjunctive is used because what
precedes is a certain verb, conjunction, or impersonal
expression. The past subjunctive is also used in relation to
a future time when another action will be completed. In
French this tense is used in formal writing and in literature
as well as in conversation and informal writing. It is a
compound tense because it is formed with the present
subjunctive of *avoir* or *être* as the auxiliary plus the past
participle of the verb you are using.

A past action in relation to the present:
Il est possible qu'elle soit partie.   / It is possible that she has left.
Je doute qu'il ait fait cela.   / I doubt that he did that.

An action that will take place in the future:
Je désire que vous soyez rentré avant dix heures.   / I want you
    to be back before ten o'clock.

§7.8–14   Pluperfect Subjunctive Tense

This tense (also called the *past perfect*) is used for the
same reasons as the imperfect subjunctive — that is, after
certain verbs, conjunctions, and impersonal expressions.
The main difference between the imperfect and the pluperfect subjunctive is the time of the action in the past. If the
action was not completed, the imperfect subjunctive is
used; if the action was completed, the pluperfect is used. In
French, it is used only in formal writing and literature.

Il était possible qu'elle fût partie. / It was possible that she might have left.

NOTE: Avoid this tense in French. Use the past subjunctive instead: *Il était possible qu'elle soit partie.*

§7.8–15 Imperative Mood

The *imperative* mood is used in French and English to express a command or request. It is also used to express an indirect request made in the third person. In both languages it is formed by dropping the subject and using the present tense. There are a few exceptions in both languages when the present subjunctive is used.

Sortez! / Get out!   *Asseyez-vous!* / Sit down!
Entrez! / Come in!   *Levez-vous!* / Get up!
Soyez à l'heure! / Be on time! (subjunctive used)
Dieu le veuille! / May God grant it! (subjunctive used)
Qu'ils mangent du gâteau! / Let them eat cake! (subjunctive used)

You must drop the final *s* in the second person singular of an *-er* verb. This is done in the affirmative and negative, as in: *Mange!* / Eat! *Ne mange pas!* / Don't eat! However, when the pronouns *y* and *en* are linked to it, the *s* is retained in all regular *-er* verbs and in the verb *aller*. The reason for this is that it makes it easier to link the two elements by pronouncing the *s* as a *z*.

Donnes-en! / Give some!
Manges-en! / Eat some!
Vas-y! / Go there!

§7.9 PASSIVE VOICE

When verbs are used in the active voice, which is almost all the time, the subject performs the action. When the *passive* voice is used, the subject of the sentence is not the performer; the action falls on the subject. The agent (the performer) is sometimes expressed, sometimes not, as is done in English. The passive voice, therefore, is composed of the verb in the passive, which is any tense of *être* + the past participle of the verb you are using to indicate the action performed upon the subject. Since *être* is the verb used in the passive voice, the past participle of your other verb must agree with the subject in gender and number.

> *Jacqueline a été reçue à l'université.* / Jacqueline has been accepted at the university.
> *Ce livre est écrit par un auteur célèbre.* / This book is written by a famous author.
> *Cette composition a été écrite par un jeune élève.* / This composition was written by a young student.

There are certain rules you must remember about the passive voice:

- Usually the preposition *de* is used instead of *par* with such verbs as *aimer, admirer, accompagner, apprécier, voir.*

> *Jacqueline est aimée de tout le monde.* / Jacqueline is liked (loved) by everyone.

> **BUT**

> *Nous avons été suivis par un chien perdu.* / We were followed by a lost dog.

- Avoid the passive voice if the thought can be expressed in the active voice with the indefinite pronoun *on* as the subject.

> *On vend de bonnes choses dans ce magasin.* / Good things are sold in this store.
> *On parle français ici.* / French is spoken here.

- You must avoid using the passive voice with a reflexive verb. Always use a reflexive verb with an active subject.

> *Elle s'appelle Jeanne.* / She is called Joan.
> *Comment se prononce ce mot?* / How is this word pronounced?

§7.10 *SI* CLAUSE: A SUMMARY

When the Verb in the *SI* clause is in the:	The Verb in the Main or Result Clause is:
present indicative	present indicative, future, or imperative
imperfect indicative	conditional
pluperfect indicative	conditional perfect

* By *si* we mean "if." Sometimes *si* can mean "whether" and in that case, this summary does not apply because there are no restrictions about the tenses. The sequence of tenses with a *si*- clause is the same in English with an "if" clause.

> *Si elle arrive, je pars.* / If she arrives, I'm leaving.
> *Si elle arrive, je partirai.* / If she arrives, I will leave.
> *Si elle arrive, partez!* / If she arrives, leave!
> *Si Paul étudiait, il aurait de meilleures notes.* / If Paul studied, he would have better grades.
> *Si Georges avait étudié, il aurait eu de bonnes notes.* / If George had studied, he would have had good grades.

§7.11 SPECIAL USES OF COMMON VERBS

DEVOIR / TO OWE; OUGHT TO

* Present

> *Je dois étudier.* / I have to study; I must study; I am supposed to study.
> *Il doit être fou!* / He must be crazy! He's probably crazy!
> *Mon père doit avoir cinquante ans.* / My father must be 50 years old.

- Imperfect

    Je devais étudier. / I had to study; I was supposed to study.
    Quand j'étais à l'école, je devais toujours étudier. / When I was in school, I always had to study.
    Ma mère devait avoir cinquante ans quand elle est morte. / My mother was probably 50 years old when she died.

- Future

    Je devrai étudier. / I will have to study.
    Nous devrons faire le travail ce soir. / We will have to do the work this evening.

- Conditional

    Je devrais étudier. / I ought to study. / I should study.
    Vous devriez étudier davantage. / You ought to study more; You should study more.

- Past indefinite

    Je ne suis pas allé(e) au cinéma parce que j'ai dû étudier. / I did not go to the movies because I had to study.
    J'ai dû prendre l'autobus parce qu'il n'y avait pas de train à cette heure-là. / I had to take the bus because there was no train at that hour.
    Robert n'est pas ici. / Robert is not here.
    Il a dû partir. / He must have left; He has probably left; He had to leave.

- Conditional perfect

    J'aurais dû étudier! / I should have studied!
    Vous auriez dû me dire la vérité. / You should have told me the truth.

- With a direct or an indirect object there is still another meaning

    Je dois de l'argent. / I owe some money.
    Je le lui dois. / I owe it to him (to her).

POUVOIR / TO BE ABLE TO, CAN

- ### Present

  Je ne peux pas sortir aujourd'hui parce que je suis malade. / I cannot (am unable to) go out today because I am sick.

  Est-ce que je peux entrer? Puis-je entrer? / May I come in?

  Madame Marin peut être malade. Mrs. Marin may be sick.

  This use of *pouvoir* suggests possibility.

  Je n'en peux plus. / I can't go on any longer.

  This use suggests physical exhaustion.

  Il se peut. / It is possible.

  This use as a reflexive verb suggests possibility.

  Cela ne se peut pas. / That can't be done.

  This use as a reflexive verb suggests impossibility.

- ### Conditional

  Pourriez-vous me prêter dix francs? / Could you lend me ten francs?

- ### Conditional perfect

  Auriez-vous pu venir chez moi? / Could you have come to my place?

  Ils auraient pu rater le train. / They might have missed the train.

VOULOIR / TO WANT

- ### Present

  Je veux aller en France. / I want to go to France.

  Je veux bien sortir avec vous ce soir. / I am willing to go out with you this evening.

Voulez-vous bien vous asseoir? / Would you be good enough to sit down?

Que veut dire ce mot? / What does this word mean?

Que voulez-vous dire? / What do you mean?

Qu'est-ce que cela veut dire? / What does that mean?

- Conditional

  Je voudrais un café crème, s'il vous plaît. / I would like coffee with cream, please.

- Imperative

  Veuillez vous asseoir. / Kindly sit down.

  Veuillez accepter mes meilleurs sentiments. / Please accept my best regards.

SAVOIR / TO KNOW (a fact)

- Present

  Je sais la réponse. / I know the answer.

  Je sais lire en français. / I know how to read in French.

- Conditional

  Sauriez-vous où est le docteur? / Would you know where the doctor is?

  Je ne saurais penser à tout! / I can't think of everything!

- Imperative

  Sachons-le bien! / Let's be well aware of it!

  Sachez que votre père vient de mourir. / Be informed that your father has just died.

SAVOIR AND *CONNAÎTRE*

The main difference between the meaning of these two verbs in the sense of "to know" is that *connaître* means merely to be acquainted with; for example, to be acquainted with a person, a city, a neighborhood, a country, the title of a book, the works of an author.

> *Savez-vous la réponse?* / Do you know the answer?
> *Savez-vous quelle heure il est?* / Do you know what time it is?
> *Connaissez-vous cette dame?* / Do you know this lady?
> *Connaissez-vous Paris?* / Do you know Paris?
> *Connaissez-vous ce livre?* / Do you know this book?

ENTENDRE AND COMPRENDRE

The main difference between the meaning of these two verbs is that *entendre* means "to hear" and *comprendre* "to understand." Sometimes *entendre* can mean "to understand" or "to mean."

> *Entendez-vous la musique?* / Do you hear the music?
> *Comprenez-vous la leçon?* / Do you understand the lesson?
> *"M'entends-tu?!" dit la mère à l'enfant. "Ne fais pas cela!"* /
>   "Do you understand me?!" says the mother to the child.
>   "Don't do that!"
> *Je ne comprends pas le docteur Fu Manchu parce qu'il ne parle que chinois.* / I do not understand Dr. Fu Manchu because he speaks only Chinese.
> *Qu'entendez-vous par là?* / What do you mean by that? What are you insinuating by that remark?
> *Je vous entends, mais je ne vous comprends pas; expliquez-vous, s'il vous plaît.* / I hear you, but I don't understand you; explain yourself, please.

QUITTER, PARTIR, SORTIR, AND LAISSER

These four verbs all mean "to leave," but note the differences in their uses:

- Use *quitter* when you state a direct object noun or pronoun that could be a person or a place.

  > *J'ai quitté mes amis devant le théâtre.* / I left my friends in front of the theater.

J'ai quitté la maison à six heures du matin. / I left the house at six in the morning.

- Use *partir* when there is no direct object noun or pronoun.

    Elle est partie tout de suite. / She left immediately.

    However, if you use the preposition *de* after *partir*, you may add a direct object, but it would be object of the preposition *de*, not of the verb *partir*.

    Elle est partie de la maison à six heures du matin. / She left (from) the house at six in the morning.

- Use *sortir*, in the sense of "to go out." With no direct object:

    Elle est sortie il y a une heure. / She went out an hour ago.

    However, if you use the preposition *de* after *sortir*, you may add a direct object, but it would be object of the preposition *de*, not of the verb *sortir*.

    Elle est sortie de la maison il y a une heure. / She left (went out of) the house an hour ago.

    Note that *sortir* can also be conjugated with *avoir* to form a compound tense, but then the meaning changes because it can take a direct object.

    Elle a sorti son mouchoir pour se moucher. / She took out her handkerchief to wipe her nose.
    Elle a sorti son mouchoir pour moucher son enfant. / She took out her handkerchief to wipe her child's nose.

- Use *laisser* when you leave behind something that is not stationary; in other words, something movable, for example, books and articles of clothing.

    J'ai laissé mes livres sur la table dans la cuisine. / I left my books on the table in the kitchen.
    J'ai laissé mon imperméable à la maison. / I left my raincoat at home.

Note that *laisser* also has the meaning "to let, allow a person to do something":

> *J'ai laissé mon ami partir.* / I let (allowed) my friend to leave.

| **Mnemonic tip** | *Partir* / to leave, go away contains an *a* and so does "away." *Sortir* / to go out contains an *o* and so does "out." |

FALLOIR

● Falloir is an impersonal verb, which means that it is used only in the third person singular (*il* form) in all the tenses; its primary meaning is "to be necessary."

> *Il faut étudier pour avoir de bonnes notes.* / It is necessary to study in order to have good grades.
> *Faut-il le faire tout de suite?* / Is it necessary to do it at once?
> *Oui, il le faut.* / Yes, it is (understood: necessary to do it).

The use of the neuter direct object *le* is needed to show emphasis and to complete the thought.

> *Il faut être honnête.* / It is necessary to be honest.

In the negative:

> *Il ne faut pas être malhonnête.* / One must not be dishonest.

Note that *il faut* in the negative means "one must not."

> *Il ne faut pas fumer à l'école.* / One must not smoke in school.

§7.12 OTHER VERBS WITH SPECIAL MEANINGS

arriver / to happen   *Qu'est-ce qui est arrivé?* / What happened?
avoir / to have something the matter   *Qu'est-ce que vous avez?* / What's the matter with you?

entendre dire que / to hear it said that, hear that *J'entends
   dire que Robert s'est marié.* / I hear that Robert got married

entendre parler de / to hear of, about *J'ai entendu parler
   d'un grand changement dans l'administration.* / I've heard
   about a big change in the administration.

envoyer chercher / to send for *Je vais envoyer chercher
   le médecin.* / I'm going to send for the doctor.

être à quelqu'un / to belong to someone *Ce livre est à
   moi.* / This book belongs to me.

faillir + infinitive to almost do something *Le bébé a failli
   tomber.* / The baby almost fell.

mettre / to put on *Gisèle a mis sa plus jolie robe.* / Gisèle
   put on her prettiest dress.

mettre la table / to set the table

profiter de / to take advantage of

rendre visite à / to pay a visit to

venir à / to happen to *Si nous venons à nous rencontrer,
   nous pourrons prendre une tasse de café.* / If we happen
   to meet each other, we can have a cup of coffee.

venir de + infinitive / to have just done something *Joseph
   vient de partir.* / Joseph has just left; *Barbara venait de
   partir quand Françoise est arrivée.* / Barbara had just left
   when Françoise arrived.

§7.13 INFINITIVES

- In English, an *infinitive* contains the preposition "to" in front
  of it: "to give," "to finish," "to sell." In French an infinitive
  has a certain ending. There are three major types of
  infinitives in French: those that end in *-er (donner);* those
  that end in *-ir (finir);* and those that end in *-re (vendre).*

- Make an infinitive negative in French by placing *ne pas* in
  front of it.

  Je vous dis de ne pas sortir. / I am telling you not to go out.

- The infinitive is often used after a verb of perception to express an action that is in progress.

    J'entends quelqu'un chanter. / I hear somebody singing.
    Je vois venir les enfants. / I see the children coming.

    Some common verbs of perception are: *apercevoir* / to perceive, *écouter* / to listen to, *entendre* / to hear, *regarder* / to look at, *sentir* / to feel, *voir* / to see.

- There are certain French verbs that take either the preposition à or de + infinitive.

    Il commence à pleuvoir. / It is beginning to rain.
    Il a cessé de pleuvoir. / It has stopped raining.

- *Avant de* and *sans* + infinitive

    Sylvie a mangé avant de sortir. / Sylvia ate before going out.
    André est parti sans dire un mot. / Andrew left without saying a word.

- Use of infinitive instead of a verb form

    Generally speaking, an infinitive is used instead of a verb form if the subject in a sentence is the same for the actions expressed.

    Je veux faire le travail. / I want to do the work.

BUT if there are two different subjects, you must use a new clause and a new verb form.

    Je veux que vous fassiez le travail. / I want you to do the work.
    Je préfère me coucher tôt. / I prefer to go to bed early.

                                    BUT

    Je préfère que vous vous couchiez tôt. / I prefer that you go to bed early.

• Past infinitive

In French the past infinitive is expressed by using the
infinitive form of *avoir* or *être* + the past participle of the
main verb being used.

*Après avoir quitté la maison, Monsieur et Madame Dubé sont
allés au cinéma.* / After leaving the house, Mr. and Mrs. Dubé
went to the movies.

Après être arrivée, Jeanne a téléphoné à sa mère. / After
arriving, Jeanne telephoned her mother.

§7.14 CAUSATIVE (CAUSAL) *FAIRE*

The construction *faire* + infinitive means to have something
done by someone. The causative *faire* can be in any tense,
but it must be followed by an infinitive.

Examples with nouns and pronouns as direct and
indirect objects:

*Madame Smith fait travailler ses élèves dans la classe de
français.* / Mrs. Smith makes her students work in French class.

In this example, the direct object is the noun *élèves* and it is
placed right after the infinitive.

Madame Smith les fait travailler dans la classe de français.
Mrs. Smith makes them work (has them work) in French class.

In this example, the direct object is the pronoun *les*, referring to *les élèves*. It is placed in front of the verb form of
faire, where it logically belongs.

Madame Smith fait lire la phrase. / Mrs. Smith is having the
sentence read. OR Mrs. Smith has the sentence read.

In this example, the direct object is the noun *phrase* and it
is placed right after the infinitive, as in the first example.

Madame Smith la fait lire. / Mrs. Smith is having it read.

In this example, the direct object is the pronoun *la*, referring to *la phrase*. It is placed in front of the verb form of *faire*, where it logically belongs. This is like the second example, but here the direct object is a thing. In the other two examples, the direct object is a person.

§7.15 SUBJUNCTIVE

The subjunctive is not a tense, but a *mood,* or mode. Usually when we speak in French or English, we use the indicative mood, but the subjunctive mood in French must be used in specific cases. They are:

After Certain Conjunctions

When the following conjunctions introduce a new clause, the verb in that new clause is usually in the subjunctive mood.

> *à condition que* / on condition that
> *à moins que* / unless
> *afin que* / in order that, so that
> *attendre que* / to wait until
> *au cas que; en cas que* / in case
> *bien que* / although
> *de crainte que* / for fear that
> *de peur que* / for fear that
> *de sorte que* / so that
> *en attendant que* / until
> *jusqu'à ce que* / until
> *malgré que* / although
> *pour que* / in order that
> *pourvu que* / provided that
> *quoique* / although

Je vous explique pour que vous compreniez. / I am explaining to you so that you will understand.

Attendez que je finisse mon dîner. / Wait until I finish my dinner.

Au cas que nous soyons d'accord . . . / In case we are in agreement . . .

En cas qu'il vienne, soyez prêts. / In case he comes, be ready.

After Indefinite Expressions

> *où que* / wherever
> *quel que* / whatever
> *qui que* / whoever
> *quoi que* / whatever, no matter what

After an Indefinite Antecedent

The subjunctive is needed after an indefinite antecedent because the person or thing desired may possibly not exist; or, if it does exist, you may never find it.

Je cherche une personne qui soit honnête. / I am looking for a person who is honest.

Je cherche un appartement qui ne soit pas trop cher. / I am looking for an apartment that is not too expensive.

Connaissez-vous quelqu'un qui puisse réparer mon téléviseur une fois pour toutes? / Do you know someone who can repair my TV set once and for all?

Y a-t-il un élève qui comprenne le subjonctif? / Is there a student who understands the subjunctive?

After a Superlative Expressing an Opinion

> The most common superlatives expressing an opinion are: *le seul (la seule)* / the only, *le premier (la première)* / the first, *le dernier (la dernière)* / the last, *le plus petit (la plus petite)* / the smallest, *le plus grand (la plus grande)* / the biggest

A mon avis, Marie est la seule étudiante qui comprenne le subjonctif. / In my opinion, Mary is the only student who understands the subjunctive.

Selon mon opinion, Henriette est l'élève la plus jolie que j'aie jamais vue. / According to my opinion, Henrietta is the prettiest pupil I have ever seen.

After *que*, Meaning "Let" or "May"

The subjunctive is required after *que* to express a wish, an order, or a command in the third person singular or plural.

Qu'il parte! / Let him leave!
Que Dieu nous pardonne! / May God forgive us!
Qu'ils s'en aillent! / Let them go away!

After Certain Impersonal Expressions

c'est dommage que / it's a pity that
il est bizarre que / it is odd that
il est bon que / it is good that
il est douteux que / it is doubtful that
il est essentiel que / it is essential that
il est étonnant que / it is astonishing that
il est étrange que / it is strange that
il est heureux que / it is fortunate that
il est honteux que / it is a shame that
il est important que / it is important that
il est impossible que / it is impossible that
il est nécessaire que / it is necessary that
il est possible que / it is possible that
il est regrettable que / it is regrettable that
il est temps que / it is time that
il est urgent que / it is urgent that
il faut que / it is necessary that
il se peut que / it may be that
il semble que / it seems that
il vaut mieux que / it is better that

After Certain Verbs Expressing Doubt, Emotion, or Wishing

aimer que / to like that
aimer mieux que / to prefer that
s'attendre à ce que / to expect that
avoir peur que / to be afraid that
craindre que / to fear that
défendre que / to forbid that
désirer que / to desire that
douter que / to doubt that
empêcher que / to prevent that
s'étonner que / to be astonished that
être bien aise que / to be pleased that
être content que / to be glad that
être désolé que / to be distressed that
être étonné que / to be astonished that
être heureux que / to be happy that
être joyeux que / to be joyful that
être ravi que / to be delighted that
être triste que / to be sad that
exiger que / to demand that
se fâcher que / to be angry that
insister que / to insist that
ordonner que / to order that
préférer que / to prefer that
regretter que / to regret that
souhaiter que / to wish that
tenir à ce que / to insist upon
vouloir que / to want

EXAMPLES

J'aimerais que vous restiez ici. / I would like you to stay here.
J'aime mieux que vous restiez ici. / I prefer that you stay here.
Nous nous attendons à ce qu'elle vienne immédiatement. / We expect her to come immediately.
Ta mère est contente que tu sois heureux. / Your mother is glad that you are happy.

After Verbs of Believing and Thinking

Such verbs are *croire, penser, trouver* (meaning "to think, to have an impression"), and *espérer* when used in the negative or interrogative.

Je ne pense pas qu'il soit coupable. / I don't think that he is guilty.
Croyez-vous qu'il dise la vérité? / Do you believe he is telling the truth?
Trouvez-vous qu'il y ait beaucoup de crimes dans la société d'aujourd'hui? / Do you find (think) that there are many crimes in today's society?

§7.16 SUMMARY OF TENSES AND MOODS

The 7 simple tenses	The 7 compound tenses
Present indicative	Past indefinite *(passé composé)*
Imperfect indicative	Pluperfect indicative
Past definite	Past anterior
Future	Future perfect
Conditional present	Conditional perfect
Present subjunctive	Past subjunctive
Imperfect subjunctive	Pluperfect subjunctive
Imperative or Command	

§7.17 SPELLING IRREGULARITIES OF SOME COMMON VERBS

The verbs conjugated here all undergo certain spelling changes in the tenses indicated.*

The subject pronouns have been omitted in order to

*For additional verb conjugations, see *French Verbs* by Christopher Kendris, ©1990 by Barron's Educational Series, Inc.

eliminate repetition and to emphasize the verb forms. They are:

	Singular	**Plural**
1st	*je (j')*	*nous*
2d	*tu*	*vous*
3d	*il, elle, on*	*ils, elles*

PRESENT INDICATIVE

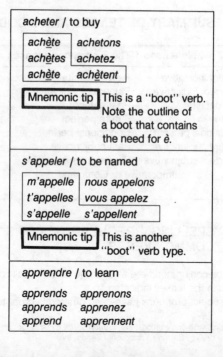

acheter / to buy

achète	achetons
achètes	achetez
achète	achètent

Mnemonic tip This is a "boot" verb. Note the outline of a boot that contains the need for *è*.

s'appeler / to be named

m'appelle	nous appelons
t'appelles	vous appelez
s'appelle	s'appellent

Mnemonic tip This is another "boot" verb type.

apprendre / to learn

apprends	apprenons
apprends	apprenez
apprend	apprennent

boire / to drink

bois	buvons
bois	buvez
boit	boivent

Mnemonic tip This too is a "boot" verb. Note the "*s, s, t*" pattern in the singular.

commencer / to begin, start

commence	commençons
commences	commencez
commence	commencent

comprendre / to understand (like *prendre*; add *com* at the beginning of *prendre*)

conduire / to drive; to lead

conduis	conduisons
conduis	conduisez
conduit	conduisent

connaître / to know, to be acquainted with

connais	connaissons
connais	connaissez
connaît	connaissent

courir / to run

cours	courons
cours	courez
court	courent

croire / to believe

crois	croyons
crois	croyez
croit	croient

devenir / to become

deviens	devenons
deviens	devenez
devient	deviennent

devoir / to owe; to have to

dois	devons
dois	devez
doit	doivent

dire / to say; to tell

dis	disons
dis	dites
dit	disent

dormir / to sleep

dors	dormons
dors	dormez
dort	dorment

écrire / to write

écris	écrivons
écris	écrivez
écrit	écrivent

envoyer / to send

envoie	envoyons
envoies	envoyez
envoie	envoient

espérer / to hope

espère	espérons
espères	espérez
espère	espèrent

falloir / to be necessary

il faut

se lever / to get up

me lève	nous levons
te lèves	vous levez
se lève	se lèvent

lire / to read

lis	lisons
lis	lisez
lit	lisent

manger / to eat

mange	mangeons
manges	mangez
mange	mangent

mettre / to place, put; to put on

mets	mettons
mets	mettez
met	mettent

mourir / to die

meurs	mourons
meurs	mourez
meurt	meurent

nager / to swim

nage	nageons
nages	nagez
nage	nagent

naître / to be born

nais	naissons
nais	naissez
naît	naissent

offrir / to offer

offre	offrons
offres	offrez
offre	offrent

ouvrir / to open

ouvre	ouvrons
ouvres	ouvrez
ouvre	ouvrent

partir / to leave

pars	partons
pars	partez
part	partent

pleuvoir / to rain

il pleut

pouvoir / to be able, can

peux OR puis	pouvons
peux	pouvez
peut	peuvent

préférer / to prefer

préf**è**re	préférons
préf**è**res	préférez
préf**è**re	préf**è**rent

prendre / to take

prends	prenons
prends	prenez
prend	prennent

protéger / to protect

prot**è**ge	protégeons
prot**è**ges	protégez
prot**è**ge	prot**è**gent

recevoir / to receive

reçoi**s**	recevons
reçoi**s**	recevez
reçoi**t**	reçoivent

revenir / to return, come back (like *venir;* add *re-* at the beginning of *venir*)

rire / to laugh

ris	rions
ris	riez
rit	rient

savoir / to know (a fact)

sais	savons
sais	savez
sait	savent

servir / to serve

sers	servons
sers	servez
sert	servent

sortir / to go out; to leave

sors	sortons
sors	sortez
sort	sortent

tenir / to hold

tiens	tenons
tiens	tenez
tient	tiennent

venir / to come

viens	venons
viens	venez
vient	viennent

vivre / to live

vis	vivons
vis	vivez
vit	vivent

voir / to see

vois	voyons
vois	voyez
voit	voient

vouloir / to want

veu<u>x</u>	voulons
veu<u>x</u>	voulez
veu<u>t</u>	veu<u>lent</u>

voyager / to travel

voyage	voyageons
voyages	voyagez
voyage	voyagent

IMPERFECT INDICATIVE

apprendre / to learn

apprenais	apprenions
apprenais	appreniez
apprenait	apprenaient

boire / to drink

bu<u>v</u>ais	bu<u>v</u>ions
bu<u>v</u>ais	bu<u>v</u>iez
bu<u>v</u>ait	bu<u>v</u>aient

commencer / to begin, to start

commen<u>ç</u>ais	commencions
commen<u>ç</u>ais	commenciez
commen<u>ç</u>ait	commen<u>ç</u>aient

comprendre / to understand (like *prendre*; add *com* at the beginning of *prendre*) *conduire* / to drive; to lead

conduisais	conduisions
conduisais	conduisiez
conduisait	conduisaient

connaître / to know, be acquainted with

connaissais	connaissions
connaissais	connaissiez
connaissait	connaissaient

courir / to run

courais	courions
courais	couriez
courait	couraient

croire / to believe

croyais	croyions
croyais	croyiez
croyait	croyaient

devenir / to become

devenais	devenions
devenais	deveniez
devenait	devenaient

devoir / to owe; to have to

devais	devions
devais	deviez
devait	devaient

dire / to say; to tell

disais	disions
disais	disiez
disait	disaient

dormir / to sleep

dormais	dormions
dormais	dormiez
dormais	dormaient

écrire / to write

écrivais	écrivions
écrivais	écriviez
écrivait	écrivaient

falloir / to be necessary

il fallait

lire / to read

lisais	lisions
lisais	lisiez
lisait	lisaient

manger / to eat

mangeais	mangions
mangeais	mangiez
mangeait	mangeaient

mourir / to die

mourais	mourions
mourais	mouriez
mourait	mouraient

nager / to swim

nageais	nagions
nageais	nagiez
nageait	nageaient

naître / to be born

naissais	*naissions*
naissais	*naissiez*
naissait	*naissaient*

offrir / to offer

offrais	*offrions*
offrais	*offriez*
offrait	*offraient*

ouvrir / to open

ouvrais	*ouvrions*
ouvrais	*ouvriez*
ouvrait	*ouvraient*

partir / to leave

partais	*partions*
partais	*partiez*
partait	*partaient*

pleuvoir / to rain

il pleuvait

prendre / to take

prenais	*prenions*
prenais	*preniez*
prenait	*prenaient*

protéger / to protect

protégeais	*protégions*
protégeais	*protégiez*
protégeait	*protégeaient*

revenir / to return, to come back
(like *venir;* add *re* at the beginning of
venir)

rire / to laugh

riais	riions
riais	riiez
riait	riaient

savoir / to know (a fact)

savais	savions
savais	saviez
savait	savaient

servir / to serve

servais	servions
servais	serviez
servait	servaient

sortir / to go out; to leave

sortais	sortions
sortais	sortiez
sortait	sortaient

tenir / to hold

tenais	tenions
tenais	teniez
tenait	tenaient

venir / to come

venais	venions
venais	veniez
venait	venaient

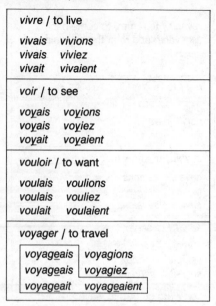

vivre / to live	
vivais	vivions
vivais	viviez
vivait	vivaient

voir / to see	
voyais	voyions
voyais	voyiez
voyait	voyaient

vouloir / to want	
voulais	voulions
voulais	vouliez
voulait	voulaient

voyager / to travel	
voyageais	voyagions
voyageais	voyagiez
voyageait	voyageaient

§7.18   BASIC NEGATIONS OF VERBS

The common negations of verbs are *ne* + verb + any of the following:

aucun, aucune / no, not one, not any

   Je n'ai aucun livre. / I have no book.
   Robert n'a aucune amie. / Robert has no girlfriend.

guère / hardly, scarcely

   Paul ne parle guère. / Paul hardly (scarcely) talks.

jamais / never

> *Jean n'étudie jamais.* / John never studies.

ni . . . ni / neither . . . nor

> *Je n'ai ni argent ni billet.* / I have neither money nor tickets.

nul, nulle / no, not any

> *Je n'en ai nul besoin.* / I have no need of it.
> *Je ne vais nulle part.* / I'm not going anywhere.

pas / not

> *Je n'ai pas de papier.* / I haven't any paper.

pas du tout / not at all

> *Je ne comprends pas du tout.* / I do not understand at all.

personne / nobody, no one, not anybody

> *Je ne vois personne.* / I don't see anybody. I see no one.

plus / any longer, no more, not any more

> *Mon père ne travaille plus.* / My father doesn't work any more.

point / not at all

> *Cet enfant n'a point d'argent.* / This child has no money at all.

que / only, but only

> *Je n'ai que deux francs.* / I have (but) only two francs.

rien / nothing

> *Je n'ai rien sur moi.* / I have nothing on me.

Note that all these negations require *ne* in front of the main verb. Also note that *aucun, aucune, nul, nulle, personne, rien* can be used as subjects and you still need to use *ne* in front of the verb.

> *Personne n'entend le bruit.* / Nobody hears the noise.
> *Rien n'est jamais parfait.* / Nothing is ever perfect.

Une devinette / a riddle

J'ai des yeux mais je n'ai pas de paupières et je vis dans l'eau. Qui suis-je? / I have eyes but I don't have eyelids and I live in the water. Who am I?

un poisson

---

§7.19   FOUR CONJUGATED VERBS

The following irregular verbs — *aller, avoir, être,* and *faire —* have been fully conjugated in all their tenses because they are so frequently used.

aller / to go
Present participle: *allant*   Past participle: *allé(e)(s)*

The Seven Simple Tenses		The Seven Compound Tenses	
Singular	**Plural**	**Singular**	**Plural**
Present indicative		Past indefinite	
vais	*allons*	*suis allé(e)*	*sommes allé(e)s*
vas	*allez*	*es allé(e)*	*êtes allé(e)(s)*
va	*vont*	*est allé(e)*	*sont allé(e)s*
Imperfect indicative		Pluperfect OR Past perfect indicative	
allais	*allions*	*étais allé(e)*	*étions allé(e)s*
allais	*alliez*	*étais allé(e)*	*étiez allé(e)(s)*
allait	*allaient*	*était allé(e)*	*étaient allé(e)s*
Past definite		Past anterior	
allai	*allâmes*	*fus allé(e)*	*fûmes allé(e)s*
allas	*allâtes*	*fus allé(e)*	*fûtes allé(e)(s)*
alla	*allèrent*	*fut allé(e)*	*furent allé(e)s*
Future		Future perfect OR Future anterior	
irai	*irons*	*serai allé(e)*	*serons allé(e)s*
iras	*irez*	*seras allé(e)*	*serez allé(e)s*
ira	*iront*	*sera allé(e)*	*seront allé(e)s*
Conditional		Conditional perfect	
irais	*irions*	*serais allé(e)*	*serions allé(e)s*
irais	*iriez*	*serais allé(e)*	*seriez allé(e)(s)*
irait	*iraient*	*serait allé(e)*	*seraient allé(e)s*
Present subjunctive		Past subjunctive	
aille	*allions*	*sois allé(e)*	*soyons allé(e)s*
ailles	*alliez*	*sois allé(e)*	*soyez allé(e)(s)*
aille	*aillent*	*soit allé(e)*	*soient allé(e)s*
Imperfect subjunctive		Pluperfect OR Past perfect subjunctive	
allasse	*allassions*	*fusse allé(e)*	*fussions allé(e)s*
allasses	*allassiez*	*fusses allé(e)*	*fussiez allé(e)(s)*
allât	*allassent*	*fût allé(e)*	*fussent allé(e)s*

Imperative OR Command
va
allons
allez

avoir / to have
Present participle: *ayant*   Past participle: *eu*

The Seven Simple Tenses		The Seven Compound Tenses	
Singular	**Plural**	**Singular**	**Plural**
Present indicative		Past indefinite	
ai	*avons*	*ai eu*	*avons eu*
as	*avez*	*as eu*	*avez eu*
a	*ont*	*a eu*	*ont eu*
Imperfect indicative		Pluperfect OR Past perfect indicative	
avais	*avions*	*avais eu*	*avions eu*
avais	*aviez*	*avais eu*	*aviez eu*
avait	*avaient*	*avait eu*	*avaient eu*
Past definite		Past anterior	
eus	*eûmes*	*eus eu*	*eûmes eu*
eus	*eûtes*	*eus eu*	*eûtes eu*
eut	*eurent*	*eut eu*	*eurent eu*
Future		Future perfect OR Future anterior	
aurai	*aurons*	*aurai eu*	*aurons eu*
auras	*aurez*	*auras eu*	*aurez eu*
aura	*auront*	*aura eu*	*auront eu*
Conditional		Conditional perfect	
aurais	*aurions*	*aurais eu*	*aurions eu*
aurais	*auriez*	*aurais eu*	*auriez eu*
aurait	*auraient*	*aurait eu*	*auraient eu*
Present subjunctive		Past subjunctive	
aie	*ayons*	*aie eu*	*ayons eu*
aies	*ayez*	*aies eu*	*ayez eu*
ait	*aient*	*ait eu*	*aient eu*
Imperfect subjunctive		Pluperfect OR Past perfect subjunctive	
eusse	*eussions*	*eusse eu*	*eussions eu*
eusses	*eussiez*	*eusses eu*	*eussiez eu*
eût	*eussent*	*eût eu*	*eussent eu*
	Imperative OR Command		
	aie		
	ayons		
	ayez		

être / to be
Present participle: *étant*   Past participle: *été*

The Seven Simple Tenses		The Seven Compound Tenses	

Singular	**Plural**	**Singular**	**Plural**
Present indicative		Past indefinite	
suis	*sommes*	*ai été*	*avons été*
es	*êtes*	*as été*	*avez été*
est	*sont*	*a été*	*ont été*
Imperfect indicative		Pluperfect OR Past perfect indicative	
étais	*étions*	*avais été*	*avions été*
étais	*étiez*	*avais été*	*aviez été*
était	*étaient*	*avait été*	*avaient été*
Past definite		Past anterior	
fus	*fûmes*	*eus été*	*eûmes été*
fus	*fûtes*	*eus été*	*eûtes été*
fut	*furent*	*eut été*	*eurent été*
Future		Future perfect OR Future anterior	
serai	*serons*	*aurai été*	*aurons été*
seras	*serez*	*auras été*	*aurez été*
sera	*seront*	*aura été*	*auront été*
Conditional		Conditional perfect	
serais	*serions*	*aurais été*	*aurions été*
serais	*seriez*	*aurais été*	*auriez été*
serait	*seraient*	*aurait été*	*auraient été*
Present subjunctive		Past subjunctive	
sois	*soyons*	*aie été*	*ayons été*
sois	*soyez*	*aies été*	*ayez été*
soit	*soient*	*ait été*	*aient été*
Imperfect subjunctive		Pluperfect OR Past perfect subjunctive	
fusse	*fussions*	*eusse été*	*eussions été*
fusses	*fussiez*	*eusses été*	*eussiez été*
fût	*fussent*	*eût été*	*eussent été*

Imperative OR Command
sois
soyons
soyez

faire / to do, to make
Present participle: *faisant*　　Past participle: *fait*

The Seven Simple Tenses		The Seven Compound Tenses	
Singular	**Plural**	**Singular**	**Plural**
Present indicative		Past indefinite	
fais	*faisons*	*ai fait*	*avons fait*
fais	*faites*	*as fait*	*avez fait*
fait	*font*	*a fait*	*ont fait*
Imperfect indicative		Pluperfect OR Past perfect indicative	
faisais	*faisions*	*avais fait*	*avions fait*
faisais	*faisiez*	*avais fait*	*aviez fait*
faisait	*faisaient*	*avait fait*	*avaient fait*
Past definite		Past anterior	
fis	*fîmes*	*eus fait*	*eûmes fait*
fis	*fîtes*	*eus fait*	*eûtes fait*
fit	*firent*	*eut fait*	*eurent fait*
Future		Future perfect OR Future anterior	
ferai	*ferons*	*aurai fait*	*aurons fait*
feras	*ferez*	*auras fait*	*aurez fait*
fera	*feront*	*aura fait*	*auront fait*
Conditional		Conditional perfect	
ferais	*ferions*	*aurais fait*	*aurions fait*
ferais	*feriez*	*aurais fait*	*auriez fait*
ferait	*feraient*	*aurait fait*	*auraient fait*
Present subjunctive		Past subjunctive	
fasse	*fassions*	*aie fait*	*ayons fait*
fasses	*fassiez*	*aies fait*	*ayez fait*
fasse	*fassent*	*ait fait*	*aient fait*
Imperfect subjunctive		Pluperfect OR Past perfect subjunctive	
fisse	*fissions*	*eusse fait*	*eussions fait*
fisses	*fissiez*	*eusses fait*	*eussiez fait*
fît	*fissent*	*eût fait*	*eussent fait*
Imperative OR Command			
fais			
faisons			
faites			

§8.

Adverbs

DEFINITION

An *adverb* is a word that modifies a verb, an adjective, or another adverb.

§8.1 FORMATION

Many French adverbs are not formed from another word, for example: *bien, mal, vite, combien, comment, pourquoi, où.*

There are many other adverbs that are formed from another word. The usual way is to add the suffix *-ment* to the masculine singular form of an adjective whose last letter is a vowel; for example: *probable, probablement; poli, poliment; vrai, vraiment.*

The suffix *-ment* is added to the feminine singular form if the masculine singular ends in a consonant; for example: *affreux, affreuse, affreusement; seul, seule, seulement; amer, amère, amèrement; franc, franche, franchement.*

The ending *-ment* is equivalent to the English ending "-ly": *lent, lente, lentement* / slow, slowly.

Some adjectives that end in *-ant* or *-ent* become adverbs by changing *-ant* to *-amment* and *-ent* to *-emment: innocent, innocemment; constant, constamment; récent, récemment.*

Some adverbs take *é* instead of *e* before adding *-ment: profond, profondément; confus, confusément; précis, précisément.*

The adjective *gentil* becomes *gentiment* as an adverb and *bref* becomes *brièvement.*

123

§8.2 POSITION

> 1. *David aime beaucoup les chocolats.*
> 2. *Paulette a parlé distinctement.*
> 3. *Julie a bien parlé.*

- In French, an adverb ordinarily follows the simple verb it modifies, as in the first model sentence above.
- If a verb is compound, as in the *past indefinite* (sentence 2), the adverb generally follows the past participle if it is a long adverb. The adverb *distinctement* is long. Some exceptions: *certainement, complètement,* and *probablement* are usually placed between the helping verb and the past participle: *Elle est probablement partie. Il a complètement fini le travail.*
- If a verb is compound, as in the *past indefinite* (sentence 3), short common adverbs (like *beaucoup, bien, déjà, encore, mal, mieux, souvent, toujours*) ordinarily precede the past participle; in other words, they may be placed between the helping verb and the past participle.
- For emphasis, an adverb may be placed at the beginning of a sentence: *Malheureusement, Suzanne est déjà partie.*

§8.3 TYPES

§8.3–1 Interrogative Adverbs

Some common interrogative adverbs are *comment, combien, pourquoi, quand, où.*

EXAMPLES
Comment allez-vous? Combien coûte ce livre? Pourquoi partez-vous? Quand arriverez-vous? Où allez-vous?

§8.3–2 Adverbs of Quantity

Some adverbial expressions of quantity are *beaucoup de, assez de, peu de, trop de, plus de.* With these, no article is used: *peu de sucre, beaucoup de travail, assez de temps, trop de lait, combien d'argent.*

§8.3–3 Comparative and Superlative Adverbs

Adverb	Comparative	Superlative
vite / quickly	*plus vite (que)* / more quickly (than) faster (than)	*le plus vite* / (the) most quickly, (the) fastest
	moins vite (que) / less quickly (than)	*le moins vite* / (the) least quickly
	aussi vite (que) / as quickly (as), as fast (as)	

EXAMPLES

Arlette parle plus vite que Marie-France. / Arlette speaks faster than Marie-France.

Madame Legrange parle moins vite que Madame Duval. / Madame Legrange speaks less quickly than Madame Duval.

Monsieur Bernard parle aussi vite que Monsieur Claude. / Monsieur Bernard speaks as fast as Monsieur Claude.

Madame Durocher parle le plus vite tandis que Madame Milot parle le moins vite. / Madame Durocher speaks the fastest whereas Madame Milot speaks the least fast (the slowest).

Aussi . . . que becomes *si . . . que* in a negative sentence.

EXAMPLE

Justin ne parle pas si vite que Justine. / Justin does not talk as fast as Justine.

Irregular Comparative and Superlative Adverbs

Adverb	Comparative	Superlative
bien / well	*mieux* / better	*le mieux* / best, the best
beaucoup / much	*plus* / more	*le plus* / most, the most
mal / badly	*plus mal* / worse *pis* / worse	*le plus mal* / worst, the worst *le moins bien* / the worst *le pis* / worst, the worst
peu / little	*moins* / less	*le moins* / least, the least

EXAMPLES
Pierre travaille bien, Henri travaille mieux que Robert et Georges travaille le mieux.
Marie étudie beaucoup, Paulette étudie plus que Marie, et Henriette étudie le plus.

§8.4 *OUI* AND *SI*

Ordinarily, *oui* is used to mean "yes." However, *si* can also be used to mean "yes" in response to a question in the negative.

EXAMPLES
Aimez-vous le français? — Oui, j'aime le français.
N'aimez-vous pas le français? — Si, j'aime le français.

> **Mnemonic tip** *Une scie* (pronounced like the English "see") is a carpenter's "saw."

§9.

Prepositions — Special Uses

§9.1 *Dans* and *en* + a length of time

The prepositions *dans* and *en* both mean "in," but each is used in a different sense.

Dans + a length of time indicates that something will happen *at the end* of that length of time.

Le docteur va venir dans une demi-heure. / The doctor will come in a half-hour (i.e., at the end of a half-hour).

Dans and a duration of time can be at the beginning of the sentence or at the end of it and future time is ordinarily implied.

En + a length of time indicates that something happened or will happen at any time *within* that length of time.

EXAMPLES
Robert a fait cela en une heure. / Robert did that in (within) an (one) hour.
Robert fera cela en une heure. / Robert will do that in (within) an (one) hour.

BUT

Robert fera cela dans une heure. / Robert will do that in (at the end of) an (one) hour.

§9.2 *Envers* and *vers*

Envers is used in a figurative sense in the meaning of "with regard to" someone, "with respect to" someone, "for" someone, or "for" something.

EXAMPLES

Je montre beaucoup de respect envers les vieilles personnes. / I
show a lot of respect toward old persons.

Je ne montre aucun respect envers un criminel. / I show no
respect toward a criminal.

Vers also means ''toward,'' but is used in the physical
sense (in the direction of) as well as in the figurative sense.

EXAMPLES

Pourquoi allez-vous vers la porte? / Why are you going toward
the door?

Je vais partir vers trois heures. / I am going to leave toward
(around) three o'clock.

§9.3 *Pendant* and *pour*

IN THE PRESENT TENSE

Combien de temps étudiez-vous chaque soir? / How long do
you study every evening?

J'étudie une heure chaque soir. / I study one hour each night.
OR *J'étudie pendant une heure chaque soir.* / I study for one
hour each night.

IN THE PAST INDEFINITE

Combien de temps êtes-vous resté(e) à Paris? / How long did
you stay in Paris?

Je suis resté(e) à Paris deux semaines. / I stayed in Paris two
weeks. OR *Je suis resté(e) à Paris pendant deux semaines.* / I
stayed in Paris for two weeks.

IN THE FUTURE

Combien de temps resterez-vous à Paris? / How long will you
stay in Paris?

J'y resterai pendant deux semaines. / I will stay there for two
weeks. OR *J'y resterai deux semaines.* / I will stay there two
weeks.

§10.

Conjunctions

§10.1 DEFINITION

A conjunction is a word that connects words, phrases, clauses, or sentences, such as *et* / and, *mais* / but, *ou* / or, *parce que* / because. The following is a list of the most common conjunctions.

§10.2 Basic Conjunctions

à moins que / unless
afin que / in order that, so that
aussitôt que / as soon as
avant que / before
bien que / although
car / for
comme / as, since
de crainte que / for fear that
de peur que / for fear that
de sorte que / so that, in such a way that
depuis que / since
dès que / as soon as
donc / therefore, consequently
en même temps que / at the same time as
et / and
jusqu'à ce que / until
lorsque / when, at the time when
maintenant que / now that
mais / but
ou / or
parce que / because
pendant le temps que / while

pendant que / while
pour que / in order that
pourvu que / provided that
puisque / since
quand / when
que / that
quoi que / whatever, no matter what
quoique / although
si / if
tandis que / while, whereas

Mnemonic tip	Pronounce the final <u>c</u> in <u>donc</u> as a *k* when it means *consequently* (therefore).

Je pense; donc, je suis, I think; therefore, I am.

Special Topics

§11.

Order of Elements in French Sentences

§11.1 Negative Constructions

Some common negative constructions are *ne* + verb + any of the following:

aucun (aucune) / no, not one, not any

> *Je n'ai aucun livre.* / I have no book.
> *Robert n'a aucune amie.* / Robert has no girlfriend.

guère / hardly, scarcely

> *Paul ne parle guère.* / Paul hardly (scarcely) talks.

jamais / never

> *Jean n'étudie jamais.* / John never studies.

ni . . . ni / neither . . . nor

> *Je n'ai ni argent ni billets.* / I have neither money nor tickets.

nul (nulle) / no, not any

> *Je n'en ai nul besoin.* / I have no need of it.
> *Je ne vais nulle part.* / I'm not going anywhere.

pas / not

> *Je n'ai pas de papier.* / I haven't any paper.

pas du tout / not at all

    Je ne comprends pas du tout. / I do not understand at all.

personne / nobody, no one, not anybody

    Je ne vois personne. / I don't see anybody. I see no one.

plus / any longer, no more, not anymore

    Mon père ne travaille plus. / My father doesn't work anymore.

point / not at all

    Cet enfant n'a point d'argent. / This child has no money at all.

que / only, but only

    Je n'ai que deux francs. / I have (but) only two francs.

rien / nothing

    Je n'ai rien sur moi. / I have nothing on me.

Remember that all these negations require *ne* in front of the main verb. Also note that *aucun (aucune)*, *nul (nulle)*, *personne*, and *rien* can be used as subjects, but you still need to use *ne* in front of the verb.

    EXAMPLES
    Personne n'est ici. / Nobody is here.
    Rien n'est dans ce tiroir. / Nothing is in this drawer.

Une devinette
J'ai des yeux mais je n'ai pas de paupières et je vis dans l'eau. Qui suis-je? / I have eyes, but I don't have eyelids and I live in the water. Who am I?

    un poisson / a fish

§11.2 Declarative Sentence with a Verb in a Simple Tense (e.g., present)

$$\textbf{SUBJECT} \rightarrow \textit{ne (n')} + \begin{Bmatrix} me\ (m') \\ te\ (t') \\ se\ (s') \\ nous \\ vous \end{Bmatrix} \text{OR} \begin{Bmatrix} le \\ la \\ l' \\ les \end{Bmatrix} \text{AND/OR} \begin{Bmatrix} lui \\ leur \end{Bmatrix}$$

$$\text{OR } y + en + \textbf{VERB} \rightarrow \textit{pas}$$

EXAMPLES

Il ne me les donne pas. / He is not giving them to me.
Je ne le leur donne pas. / I am not giving it to them.
Il n'y en a pas. / There aren't any of them.

§11.3 Declarative Sentence with a Verb in a Compound Tense (e.g., *passé composé*)

$$\textbf{SUBJECT} \rightarrow \textit{ne (n')} + \begin{Bmatrix} me\ (m') \\ te\ (t') \\ se\ (s') \\ nous \\ vous \end{Bmatrix} \text{OR} \begin{Bmatrix} le \\ la \\ l' \\ les \end{Bmatrix} \text{AND/OR} \begin{Bmatrix} lui \\ leur \end{Bmatrix}$$

$$\text{OR } y + en + \textbf{VERB} \rightarrow \textit{pas} +$$

past participle
(auxiliary verb
avoir or *être* in
a simple tense)

EXAMPLES

Yvonne ne s'est pas lavée. / Yvonne did not wash herself.
Il ne m'en a pas envoyé. / He did not send any of them to me.
Je ne le lui ai pas donné. / I did not give it to him (to her).
Nous ne vous les avons pas données. / We have not given them to you.
Ils ne s'en sont pas allés. / They did not go away.

§11.4 Affirmative Imperative Sentence

$$\text{VERB} + \begin{Bmatrix} le \\ la \\ l' \\ les \end{Bmatrix} \text{ OR } \begin{Bmatrix} moi\ (m') \\ toi\ (t') \\ nous \\ vous \end{Bmatrix} \text{ AND/OR } \begin{Bmatrix} lui \\ leur \end{Bmatrix} \text{ OR } y + en$$

EXAMPLES

Donnez-les-leur. / Give them to them.
Assieds-toi. / Sit down.
Allez-vous-en! / Go away!
Apportez-le-moi! / Bring it to me!
Donnez-m'en! / Give me some!
Allez-y! / Go to it! Go there!

§11.5 Negative Imperative Sentence

$$\text{Ne (N')} + \begin{Bmatrix} me\ (m') \\ te\ (t') \\ nous \\ vous \end{Bmatrix} \text{ OR } \begin{Bmatrix} le \\ la \\ l' \\ les \end{Bmatrix} \text{ OR } \begin{Bmatrix} lui \\ leur \end{Bmatrix} \text{ OR } y + en + \text{VERB} \rightarrow pas$$

EXAMPLES

Ne l'y mettez pas. / Do not put it in it. Do not put it there.
Ne les leur donnez pas. / Do not give them to them.
Ne t'assieds pas! / Don't sit down!
Ne vous en allez pas! / Don't go away!

| Mnemonic tip | Object pronouns fall in the right order if you alphabetize them! |

$$\begin{matrix} \left.\begin{matrix} la \\ le \\ les \end{matrix}\right\} & + & \begin{matrix} leur \\ \\ lui \end{matrix} \end{matrix}$$

The order is always the same, whether before or after a verb or before an infinitive.

§12.

Idioms

§12.1 SPECIAL USES

Depuis

With the present indicative tense

When an action of some sort began in the past and is still going on in the present, use the present tense with *depuis* + the length of time.

Je travaille dans ce bureau depuis trois ans. / I have been working in this office for three years.

> Use *depuis combien de temps* + the present indicative of the verb to ask how long one has been + verb: *Depuis combien de temps travaillez-vous dans ce bureau?* / How long have you been working in this office? *Je travaille dans ce bureau depuis un an.* / I have been working in this office for one year.

With the imperfect indicative tense

When an action of some sort began in the past and continued up to another point in the past that you are telling about, use the imperfect indicative tense with depuis + the length of time:

J'attendais l'autobus depuis vingt minutes quand il est arrivé. / I had been waiting for the bus for twenty minutes when it arrived.

• In a question

> *Depuis combien de temps attendez-vous l'autobus?* / How long
> have you been waiting for the bus?
> *J'attends l'autobus depuis vingt minutes.* / I have been waiting
> for the bus for twenty minutes.

Note: When you use *depuis combien de temps* in a
question, you expect the other person to tell you how
long, how much time—how many minutes, how many
hours, how many days, weeks, months, years, etc.

> *Depuis quand habitez-vous cet appartement?* / Since when have
> you been living in this apartment?
> *J'habite cet appartement depuis le premier septembre.* / I have
> been living in this apartment since September first.

Note: When you use *depuis quand* in your question, you
expect the other person to tell you since what particular
point in time in the past—a particular day, date, month;
in other words, since *when*, not *how long.*

> *Depuis quand êtes-vous malade?* / Since when have you been
> sick?
> *Je suis malade depuis samedi.* / I have been sick since Saturday.
> *Depuis quand habitiez-vous l'appartement quand vous avez
> déménagé?* / Since when had you been living in the apartment
> when you moved?
> *J'habitais l'appartement depuis le cinq avril dernier quand j'ai
> déménagé.* / I had been living in the apartment since last
> April fifth when I moved.

Il y a + Length of Time + *que; voici* + Length of
Time + *que; voilà* + Length of Time + *que*

• In questions and answers

> *Depuis combien de temps attendez-vous l'autobus?* / How long
> have you been waiting for the bus?
> *J'attends l'autobus depuis vingt minutes.* / I have been waiting
> for the bus for twenty minutes.

Voici vingt minutes que je l'attends. / I have been waiting for it
   for twenty minutes.
Voilà vingt minutes que je l'attends. / I have been waiting for it
   for twenty minutes.

Note: When you use these expressions, you generally
use them at the beginning of your answer + the verb.
   When you use the *depuis* construction, the verb
comes first: *J'attends l'autobus depuis vingt minutes.*

y a + length of time

   Il y a + length of time means "ago." Do not use *que* in
this construction as in the above examples because the
meaning is entirely different.

Madame Martin est partie il y a une heure. / Mrs. Martin left an
   hour ago.
L'autobus est arrivé il y a vingt minutes. / The bus arrived
   twenty minutes ago.

y a and *Il y avait*

   Il y a alone means "there is" or "there are" when you
are merely making a statement.

Il y a vingt élèves dans cette classe. / There are twenty
   students in this class.
Il y a une mouche dans la soupe. / There is a fly in the soup.

y avait alone means "there was" or "there were" when
you are merely making a statement.

Il y avait vingt élèves dans cette classe. / There were (used to
   be) twenty students in this class.
Il y avait deux mouches dans la soupe. / There were two flies in
   the soup.

Voici and *Voilà*

These two expressions are used to point out someone or
something.

Voici un taxi! / Here's a taxi!

Voilà un taxi là-bas! / There's a taxi over there!

Voici ma carte d'identité et voilà mon passeport. / Here's my ID
card and there's my passport.

Voici mon père et voilà ma mère. / Here's my father and there's
my mother.

§12.2 BASIC EXPRESSIONS

With *à*

à bicyclette / by bicycle, on a bicycle	*à l'heure* / on time
à bientôt / so long, see you soon	*à l'instant* / instantly
	à l'occasion / on the occasion
à cause de / on account of, because of	*à la campagne* / at (in, to) the country(side)
à cette heure / at this time, at the present moment	*à la fin* / at last, finally
	à la fois / at the same time
à cheval / on horseback	*à la main* / in one's hand, by hand
à côté de / beside, next to	*à la maison* / at home
à demain / until tomorrow, see you tomorrow	*à la mode* / fashionable, in style, in fashion
à droite / at (on, to) the right	*à la radio* / on the radio
à gauche / at (on, to) the left	*à la recherche de* / in search of
	à la télé / on TV
à haute voix / aloud, out loud, in a loud voice	*à mon avis* / in my opinion
	à part / aside
à jamais / forever	*à partir de* / beginning with
à l'école / at (in, to) school	*à peine* / hardly, scarcely
à l'étranger / abroad, overseas	*à peu près* / approximately, about, nearly

à *pied* / on foot
à *plus tard* / see you later
à *présent* / now, at present
à *propos* / by the way
à *propos de* / about, with reference to, concerning
à *quelle heure?* / at what time?
à *qui est ce livre?* / whose is this book?
à *quoi bon?* / what's the use?
à *son gré* / to one's liking
à *temps* / in time

à *tour de rôle* / in turn
à *tout à l'heure* / see you in a little while
à *tout prix* / at any cost
à *travers* / across, through
à *tue-tête* / at the top of one's voice, as loud as possible

à *vélo* / on a bike
à *voix basse* / in a low voice, softly
à *volonté* / at will, willingly
à *vrai dire* / to tell the truth
à *vue d'œil* / visibly

With *au*

au bas de / at the bottom of
au besoin / if need be, if necessary
au bout de / at the end of, at the tip of
au contraire / on the contrary
au début / at (in) the beginning
au-dessous de / below, beneath
au-dessus de / above, over
au fond de / in the bottom of
au haut de / at the top of
au lieu de / instead of

au milieu de / in the middle of
au moins / at least
au pied de / at the foot of
au printemps / in the spring
au revoir / goodbye
au sous-sol / in the basement
au sujet de / about, concerning
au téléphone / on the telephone
café au lait / coffee with milk
rosbif au jus / roast beef with gravy

With *aux*

aux dépens / at the expense	*rire aux éclats* / to roar with laughter
aux pommes frites / with French fries	*sauter aux yeux* / to be evident, self-evident

With *aller*

aller / to feel (health): *Comment allez-vous?*

aller à / to be becoming, fit, suit: *Cette robe lui va bien.* / This dress suits her fine. *Sa barbe ne lui va pas.* / His beard does not look good on him.

aller à la chasse / to go hunting

aller à la pêche / to go fishing

aller à la rencontre de quelqu'un / to go to meet someone

aller à pied / to walk, go on foot

aller au fond des choses / to get to the bottom of things

aller chercher / to go get

allons donc! / nonsense! come on, now!

With *avoir*

avoir . . . ans / to be . . . years old: *Quel âge — avez-vous?* / J'ai dix-sept ans.

avoir à + infinitive / to have to

avoir affaire à quelqu'un / to deal with someone

avoir beau + infinitive / to be useless + infinitive, to do something in vain: *Vous avez beau parler; je ne vous écoute pas.* / You are talking in vain; I am not listening to you.

avoir besoin de / to need, to have need of

avoir bonne mine / to look well

avoir chaud / to be (feel) warm (persons)

avoir congé / to have a day off, a holiday

avoir de la chance / to be lucky

avoir de quoi + infinitive / to have the material, means, enough + infinitive: *As-tu de quoi manger?* / Have you something (enough) to eat?

avoir des nouvelles / to receive news

avoir du savoir-faire / to have tact

avoir du savoir-vivre / to have good manners

avoir envie de + infinitive / to have a desire to

avoir faim / to be (feel) hungry

avoir froid / to be (feel) cold (persons)

avoir hâte / to be in a hurry

avoir honte / to be ashamed, to feel ashamed

avoir l'air + adjective / to seem, to look + adjective: *Vous avez l'air malade.* / You look sick.

avoir l'air de + infinitive / to appear + infinitive: *Vous avez l'air d'être malade.* / You appear to be sick.

avoir l'habitude de + infinitive / to be accustomed to, to be in the habit of: *J'ai l'habitude de faire mes devoirs avant le dîner.* / I'm in the habit of doing my homework before dinner.

avoir l'idée de + infinitive / to have a notion + infinitive

avoir l'intention de + infinitive / to intend + infinitive

avoir la bonté de + infinitive / to have the kindness

avoir la langue bien pendue / to have the gift of gab

avoir la parole / to have the floor (to speak)

avoir le cœur gros / to be heartbroken

avoir le temps de + infinitive / to have (the) time + infinitive

avoir lieu / to take place

avoir mal / to feel sick

avoir mal à + (place where it hurts) / to have a pain or ache in . . . : *J'ai mal à la jambe.* / My leg hurts. *J'ai mal au dos.* / My back hurts. *J'ai mal au cou.* / I have a pain in the neck.

avoir mauvaise mine / to look ill, not to look well

avoir peine à + infinitive / to have difficulty in + present participle

avoir peur de / to be afraid of

avoir pitié de / to take pity on

avoir raison / to be right (persons)

avoir soif / to be thirsty

avoir sommeil / to be sleepy

avoir son mot à dire / to have one's way

avoir tort / to be wrong (persons)

avoir une faim de loup / to be starving

With *bas*

au bas de / at the bottom of

en bas / downstairs, below

là-bas / over there

A bas les devoirs! / Down with homework!

parler tout bas / to speak very softly

de haut en bas / from top to bottom

With *bien*

bien des / many: *Roger a bien des amis.* / Roger has many friends.
bien entendu / of course
dire du bien de / to speak well of

être bien aise / to be very glad, happy
tant bien que mal / rather badly, so-so

With *bon*

à quoi bon? / what's the use?
bon gré, mal gré / willing or not, willy nilly
bon marché / cheap, at a low price
bon pour quelqu'un / good to someone

de bon appétit / with good appetite, heartily
de bon cœur / gladly, willingly
savoir bon gré à quelqu'un / to be thankful, grateful to someone

With *ça*

çà et là / here and there
Ça m'est égal. / It makes no difference to me.
comme ci, comme ça / so-so

Ça va? / Is everything okay?
C'est comme ça! / That's how it is!
Pas de ça! / None of that!

With *cela*

Cela est égal. / It's all the same. It doesn't matter. It makes no difference.

Cela m'est égal. / It doesn't matter to me. It's all the same to me.

Cela n'importe. / That doesn't matter.

Cela ne fait rien. / That makes no difference.

Cela ne sert à rien. / That serves no purpose.

Cela ne vous regarde pas. / That's none of your business.

malgré cela / in spite of that

malgré tout cela / in spite of all that

Qu'est-ce que cela veut dire? / What does that mean?

With *ce, c'est, est-ce*

c'est-à-dire / that is, that is to say

C'est aujourd'hui lundi. / Today is Monday.

C'est dommage. / It's a pity. It's too bad.

C'est entendu. / It's understood. It's agreed. All right. OK.

C'est épatant! / It's wonderful!

C'est trop fort! / That's just too much!

n'est-ce pas? / isn't that so? isn't it?, etc.

Qu'est-ce que c'est? / What is it?

Quel jour est-ce aujourd'hui? / What day is it today? *C'est lundi.* / It's Monday.

Qu'est-ce qui s'est passé? / What happened?

With *d'*

changer d'avis / to change one's opinion, one's mind	*d'avance* / in advance, beforehand
comme d'habitude / as usual	*d'habitude* / ordinarily, usually, generally
d'abord / at first	*d'ici longtemps* / for a long time to come
d'accord / okay, agreed	*d'ordinaire* / ordinarily, usually, generally
d'ailleurs / besides, moreover	*tout d'un coup* / all of a sudden
d'aujourd'hui en huit / a week from today	

With *de*

au haut de / at the top of	*de nouveau* / again
autour de / around	*de parti pris* / on purpose, deliberately
changer de train / to change trains: *changer de vêtements* / to change clothes	*de plus* / furthermore
combien de / how much, how many	*de plus en plus* / more and more
de bon appétit / with good appetite, heartily	*de quelle couleur . . . ?* / what color . . . ?
de bon cœur / gladly, willingly	*de quoi* + infinitive / something, enough + infinitive: *de quoi écrire* / something to write with; *de quoi manger* / something or enough to eat; *de quoi vivre* / something or enough to live on
de bonne heure / early	
de cette façon / in this way	
de jour en jour / from day to day	
de l'autre côté de / on the other side of	
de la part de / on behalf of, from	*de rien* / you're welcome, don't mention it

de rigueur / required, obligatory

de son mieux / one's best

de suite / one after another, in succession

de temps en temps / from time to time, occasionally

de toutes ses forces / with all one's might, strenuously

du côté de / in the direction of, toward

éclater de rire / to burst out laughing

en face de / opposite

entendre parler de / to hear about

être de retour / to be back

être en train de / to be in the act of, in the process of

être temps de + infinitive / to be time + infinitive

faire semblant de + infinitive / to pretend + infinitive

féliciter quelqu'un de quelque chose / to congratulate someone for something

Il n'y a pas de quoi! / You're welcome!

jamais de la vie! / never in one's life! never! out of the question!

jouer de / to play (a musical instrument)

manquer de + infinitive / to fail to, to almost do something: *Victor a manqué de se noyer.* / Victor almost drowned.

mettre de côté / to lay aside, to save

pas de mal! / no harm!

près de / near

quelque chose de + adjective / something + adjective: *J'ai bu quelque chose de bon!* / I drank something good!

Quoi de neuf? / What's new?

Rien de neuf! / Nothing's new!

tout de même / all the same

tout de suite / immediately, at once

venir de + infinitive / to have just done something; *Je viens de manger.* / I have just eaten.

With *du*

dire du bien de quelqu'un / to speak well of someone

dire du mal de quelqu'un / to speak ill of someone

donner du chagrin à quelqu'un / to give someone grief

du côté de / in the direction of, toward

du matin au soir / from morning until night

du moins / at least

du reste / besides, in addition, furthermore

montrer du doigt / to point out, to show, to indicate by pointing

pas du tout / not at all

With *en*

de jour en jour / from day to day

de temps en temps / from time to time

en anglais, en français, etc. / in English, in French, etc.

en arrière / backwards, to the rear, behind

en automne, en hiver, en été / in the fall, in winter, in summer

en automobile / by car

en avion / by plane

en avoir plein le dos / to be sick and tired of something

en bas / downstairs, below

en bateau / by boat

en bois, en pierre, en + a material / made of wood, of stone, etc.

en chemin de fer / by train

en dessous (de) / underneath

en dessus (de) / above, on top, over

en effet / in fact, indeed, yes, indeed

en face de / opposite

en famille / as a family

en haut / upstairs, above

en huit jours / in a week

en même temps / at the same time

en panne / mechanical breakdown

en plein air / in the open air, outdoors

en retard / late, not on time

en tout cas / in any case, at any rate

en toute hâte / with all possible speed, haste

en ville / downtown, in (at, to) town

En voilà assez! / Enough of that!

en voiture / by car: *en voiture!* / all aboard!

être en train de + infinitive / to be in the act of + present participle, to be in the process of, to be busy + present participle

Je vous en prie. / I beg you. You're welcome.

mettre en pièces / to tear to pieces, to break into pieces

voir tout en rose / to see the bright side of things, to be optimistic

With *être*

être à l'heure / to be on time

être à quelqu'un / to belong to someone: *Ce livre est à moi.* / This book belongs to me.

être au courant de / to be informed about

être bien / to be comfortable

être d'accord avec / to agree with

être de retour / to be back

être en retard / to be late, not to be on time

être en train de + infinitive / to be in the act of, to be in the process of, to be busy + present participle

être en vacances / to be on vacation

être enrhumé / to have a cold, be sick with a cold

être pressé(e) / to be in a hurry

Quelle heure est-il? / What time is it? *Il est une heure.* / It is one o'clock. *Il est deux heures.* / It is two o'clock

With *faire*

Cela ne fait rien. / That doesn't matter.

Comment se fait-il? / How come?

faire à sa tête / to have one's way

faire attention (à) / to pay attention (to)

faire beau / to be pleasant, nice weather

faire bon accueil / to welcome

faire chaud / to be warm (weather)

faire de l'autostop / to hitchhike

faire de son mieux / to do one's best

faire des châteaux en Espagne / to build castles in the air

faire des emplettes; faire des courses; faire du shopping / to do or to go shopping

faire des progrès / to make progress

faire du bien à quelqu'un / to do good for someone

faire du vélo / to ride a bike

faire exprès / to do on purpose

faire face à / to oppose

faire froid / to be cold (weather)

faire jour / to be daylight

faire la bête / to act like a fool

faire la connaissance de quelqu'un / to make the acquaintance of someone, meet someone for the first time

faire la cuisine / to do the cooking

faire la grasse matinée / to sleep late in the morning

faire la lessive / to do the laundry

faire (une) la malle / to pack (a) the trunk

faire la queue / to line up, to get in line, to stand in line

faire la vaisselle / to do (wash) the dishes

faire le ménage / to do housework

faire les bagages / to pack the baggage, luggage

faire les valises / to pack the suitcases, valises

faire mal à quelqu'un / to hurt, to harm someone

faire nuit / to be night(time)

faire peur à quelqu'un / to frighten someone

faire plaisir à quelqu'un / to please someone

faire sa toilette / to wash and dress oneself

faire ses adieux / to say goodbye

faire son possible / to do one's best

faire suivre le courrier / to forward mail

faire un tour / to go for a stroll

faire un voyage / to take a trip

faire une partie de / to play a game of

faire une promenade / to take a walk

faire une visite / to pay a visit

faire venir quelqu'un / to have someone come: *Il a fait venir le docteur.* / He had the doctor come.

faire venir l'eau à la bouche / to make one's mouth water

Faites comme chez vous! / Make yourself at home!

Que faire? / What is to be done?

Quel temps fait-il? / What's the weather like?

With *mieux*

aimer mieux / to prefer, like better

aller mieux / to feel better (person's health): *Êtes-vous toujours malade?* / Are you still sick? *Je vais mieux, merci.* / I'm feeling better, thank you.

de son mieux / one's best

faire de son mieux / to do one's best

tant mieux / so much the better

valoir mieux / to be better (worth more), to be preferable

With *non*

> *Je crois que non.* / I don't think so.
> *Mais non!* / Of course not!
> *Non merci!* / No, thank you!
>
> *J'espère bien que non.* / I hope not.

With *par*

> *par bonheur* / fortunately
> *par-ci; par-là* / here and there
> *par conséquent* / consequently, therefore
> *par exemple* / for example
> *par hasard* / by chance
> *par ici* / through here, this way, in this direction
> *par jour* / per day, daily
> *par la fenêtre* / out, through the window
> *par-là* / through there, that way, in that direction
> *par malheur* / unfortunately
> *par mois* / per month, monthly
>
> *par semaine* / per week, weekly
> *par tous les temps* / in all kinds of weather
> *apprendre par cœur* / to learn by heart, memorize
> *finir par* + infinitive / to end up + present participle: *Ils ont fini par se marier.* / They ended up by getting married.
> *jeter l'argent par la fenêtre* / to waste money

With *plus*

de plus / furthermore, besides, in addition
de plus en plus / more and more
n'en pouvoir plus / to be exhausted, not to be able to go on any longer: *Je n'en peux plus!* / I can't go on any longer!

Plus ça change plus c'est la même chose. / The more it changes, the more it remains the same.
une fois de plus / once more, one more time

With *quel*

Quel âge avez-vous? / How old are you?
Quel garçon! / What a boy!

Quel jour est-ce aujourd'hui? / What day is it today?

With *quelle*

De quelle couleur est (sont) . . . ? / What color is (are) . . . ?
Quelle fille! / What a girl!

Quelle heure est-il? / What time is it?
Quelle chance! / What luck!

With *quelque chose*

quelque chose à +
infinitive / something
+ infinitive: *J'ai
quelque chose à lui
dire.* / I have some-
thing to say to him (to
her).

quelque chose de +
adjective / something +
adjective: *J'ai quelque
chose d'intéressant à
vous dire.* / I have
something interesting to
tell you.

With *quoi*

à quoi bon? / what's the
use?
avoir de quoi + infinitive /
to have something
(enough) + infinitive:
*Avez-vous de quoi
écrire?* / Do you have
something to write
with?

avoir de quoi manger / to
have something to eat
Il n'y a pas de quoi! /
You're welcome!
Quoi de neuf? / What's
new?

With *rien*

Cela ne fait rien. / That
doesn't matter.
Cela ne sert à rien. / That
serves no purpose.

de rien / you're welcome,
don't mention it
Rien de neuf! / Nothing's
new!

With *tant*

tant bien que mal / so-so	*Je t'aime tant!* / I love you so much!
tant mieux / so much the better	
tant pis / so much the worse	*tant de choses* / so many things
J'ai tant de travail! / I have so much work!	

With *tous*

tous (les) deux / both (m. plural)	*tous les soirs* / every evening
tous les ans / every year	*tous les mois* / every month
tous les jours / every day	
tous les matins / every morning	

With *tout*

après tout / after all	*tout d'un coup* / all of a sudden
en tout cas / in any case, at any rate	
pas du tout / not at all	*tout de même!* / all the same! just the same!
tout à coup / suddenly	
tout à fait / completely, entirely	*tout de suite* / immediately, at once, right away
tout à l'heure / a little while ago, in a little while	
tout d'abord / first of all	*tout le monde* / everybody
	tout le temps / all the time

With *toute*

en toute hâte / with all possible speed, in great haste *toute chose* / everything *de toutes ses forces* / with all one's might	*toutes (les) deux* / both (f. plural) *toutes les nuits* / every night

With *y*

il y a + length of time / ago: *il y a un mois* / a month ago *il y a* / there is, there are *il y avait . . .* / there was (there were) . . .	*Il n'y a pas de quoi.* / You're welcome. *y compris* / including

§13.

Dates, Days, Months, Seasons

§13.1 Dates

Quelle est la date aujourd'hui? / What's the date today?
Quel jour sommes-nous aujourd'hui? / What's the date today?

C'est aujourd'hui le premier octobre. / Today is October first
C'est aujourd'hui le deux novembre. / Today is November second.

C'est lundi. / It's Monday.
C'est aujourd'hui mardi. / Today is Tuesday.

Quand êtes-vous né(e)? / When were you born?
Je suis né(e) le vingt-deux août, mil neuf cent soixante-six.
I was born on August 22, 1966.

Use the cardinal numbers for dates, except "the first," which is *le premier*.

§13.2 Days

The days of the week, which are all masculine, are:

dimanche / Sunday	*jeudi* / Thursday
lundi / Monday	*vendredi* / Friday
mardi / Tuesday	*samedi* / Saturday
mercredi / Wednesday	

§13.3 Months

The months of the year, which are all masculine, are:

janvier / January	*juillet* / July
février / February	*août* / August
mars / March	*septembre* / September
avril / April	*octobre* / October
mai / May	*novembre* / November
juin / June	*décembre* / December

To say "in" + the name of the month, use *en: en janvier, en février;* OR *au mois de janvier, au mois de février* / in the month of January, etc.

§13.4 Seasons

The seasons of the year, which are all masculine, are:

le printemps / spring	*l'automne* / fall
l'été / summer	*l'hiver* / winter

| Mnemonic tip | *En hiver,* you shiver.

To say "in" + the name of the season, use *en* except with *printemps: au printemps, en été, en automne, en hiver* / in spring, in summer, etc.

§14.

Telling Time

§14.1 TIME EXPRESSIONS YOU OUGHT TO KNOW

Quelle heure est-il? / What time is it?
Il est une heure. / It is one o'clock.
Il est une heure dix. / It is ten minutes after one.
Il est une heure et quart. / It is a quarter after one.
Il est deux heures et demie. / It is half past two; it is two thirty.
Il est trois heures moins vingt. / It is twenty minutes to three.
Il est trois heures moins le quart. / It is a quarter to three.
Il est midi. / It is noon.
Il est minuit. / It is midnight.
à quelle heure? / at what time?
à une heure / at one o'clock
à une heure précise / at exactly one o'clock
à deux heures précises / at exactly two o'clock
à neuf heures du matin / at nine in the morning
à trois heures de l'après-midi / at three in the afternoon
à dix heures du soir / at ten in the evening
à l'heure / on time
à temps / in time
vers trois heures / around three o'clock; about three o'clock
un quart d'heure / a quarter of an hour; a quarter hour
une demi-heure / a half hour

> *Il est midi et demi* / It is twelve thirty; It is half past
> twelve (noon).
>
> *Il est minuit et demi.* / It is twelve thirty; It is half past
> twelve (midnight).

- In telling time, *Il est* + the hour is used, whether it is one or
  more than one, e.g., *Il est une heure. Il est deux heures.*

- If the time is after the hour, state the hour, then the minutes:
  Il est une heure dix.

- The conjunction *et* is used with *quart* after the hour and
  with *demi* or *demie: Il est une heure et quart. Il est une
  heure et demie. Il est midi et demi.*

  The masculine form *demi* is used after a masculine noun:
  Il est midi et demi. The feminine form *demie* is used after a
  feminine noun: *Il est deux heures et demie.*

  Demi remains *demi* when before a feminine or masculine
  noun, and is joined to the noun with a hyphen: *une demi-heure.*

- If the time expressed is before the hour, *moins* is used: *Il
  est trois heures moins vingt.*

- A quarter to the hour is *moins le quart.*

- To express A.M. use *du matin;* to express P.M. use *de
  l'après-midi* if the time is in the afternoon; *du soir* if in the
  evening.

§14.2 "OFFICIAL" TIME EXPRESSIONS

Another way to tell time is the official time used by the
French government on radio and TV, in railroad and bus
stations, and at airports.

- It is the twenty-four-hour system.

- In this system, *quart, demi, demie, moins,* and *et* are not used.

• When you hear or see the stated time, subtract twelve from the number you hear or see. If the number is less than twelve, it is A.M. time, except for *24 heures,* which is midnight; *zéro heure* is also midnight.

EXAMPLES

> *Il est treize heures.* / It is 1:00 P.M.
> *Il est quinze heures.* / It is 3:00 P.M.
> *Il est vingt heures trente.* / It is 8:30 P.M.
> *Il est minuit.* / It is midnight.
> *It est seize heures trente.* / It is 4:30 P.M.
> *Il est dix-huit heures quinze.* / It is 6:15 P.M.
> *Il est vingt heures quarante-cinq.* / It is 8:45 P.M.
> *Il est vingt-deux heures cinquante.* / It is 10:50 P.M.

The abbreviation for *heure* or *heures* is *h.*

EXAMPLES

> *Il est 20 h. 20.* / It is 8:20 P.M.
> *Il est 15 h. 50.* / It is 3:50 P.M.
> *Il est 23 h. 30.* / It is 11:30 P.M.

§15.

Talking About the Weather

Quel temps fail-il? / What's the weather like?

WITH *Il fait . . .*

Il fait beau. / The weather is fine. The weather is beautiful.
Il fait beau temps. / The weather is beautiful.
Il fait chaud. / It's warm.
Il fait clair. / It is clear.
Il fait doux. / It's mild.
Il fait du soleil. / It's sunny. (You can also say *Il fait soleil.*)
Il fait du tonnerre. / It's thundering. (OR: *Il tonne.*)
Il fait du vent. / It's windy.
Il fait frais. / It is cool.
Il fait froid. / It's cold.
Il fait humide. / It's humid.
Il fait mauvais. / The weather is bad.

WITH *Il fait un temps . . .*

Il fait un temps affreux. / The weather is frightful.
Il fait un temps calme. / The weather is calm.
Il fait un temps couvert. / The weather is cloudy.
Il fait un temps lourd. / It's muggy.
Il fait un temps magnifique. / The weather is magnificent.
Il fait un temps superbe. / The weather is superb.

WITH *Le temps + VERB . . .*

Le temps menace. / The weather is threatening.
Le temps se gâte. / The weather is getting bad.
Le temps se met au beau. / The weather is getting beautiful.
Le temps se met au froid. / It's getting cold.
Le temps se rafraîchit. / The weather is getting cool.

161

WITH *Le ciel est* . . .

Le ciel est bleu. / The sky is blue.
Le ciel est calme. / The sky is calm.
Le ciel est couvert. / The sky is cloudy.
Le ciel est gris. / The sky is gray.

WITH OTHER VERBS

Il gèle. / It's freezing.
Il grêle. / It's hailing.
Il neige. / It's snowing.
Il pleut. / It's raining.
Il tombe de la grêle. / It's hailing.

§16.

Numbers

Cardinal Numbers: 1 to 1000

0 *zéro*	40 *quarante*
1 *un, une*	41 *quarante et un*
2 *deux*	42 *quarante-deux*, etc.
3 *trois*	
4 *quatre*	50 *cinquante*
5 *cinq*	51 *cinquante et un*
6 *six*	52 *cinquante-deux*, etc.
7 *sept*	
8 *huit*	60 *soixante*
9 *neuf*	61 *soixante et un*
10 *dix*	62 *soixante-deux*, etc.
11 *onze*	
12 *douze*	70 *soixante-dix*
13 *treize*	71 *soixante et onze*
14 *quatorze*	72 *soixante-douze*, etc.
15 *quinze*	
16 *seize*	80 *quatre-vingts*
17 *dix-sept*	81 *quatre-vingt-un*
18 *dix-huit*	82 *quatre-vingt-deux*, etc.
19 *dix-neuf*	
	90 *quatre-vingt-dix*
20 *vingt*	91 *quatre-vingt-onze*
21 *vingt et un*	92 *quatre-vingt-douze*,
22 *vingt-deux*, etc.	etc.
30 *trente*	100 *cent*
31 *trente et un*	101 *cent un*
32 *trente-deux*, etc.	102 *cent deux*, etc.

200 *deux cents* 201 *deux cent un* 202 *deux cent deux*, etc.	800 *huit cents* 801 *huit cent un* 802 *huit cent deux*, etc.
300 *trois cents* 301 *trois cent un* 302 *trois cent deux*, etc.	900 *neuf cents* 901 *neuf cent un* 902 *neuf cent deux*, etc.
400 *quatre cents* 401 *quatre cent un* 402 *quatre cent deux*, etc.	1000 *mille*
500 *cinq cents* 501 *cinq cent un* 502 *cinq cent deux*, etc.	
600 *six cents* 601 *six cent un* 602 *six cent deux*, etc.	Mnemonic tip If you're not sure that *vingt* is spelled with *ng* or *gn*, note this:
700 *sept cents* 701 *sept cent un* 702 *sept cent deux*, etc.	$$\begin{array}{ccccc} V & I & \boxed{N} & G & T \\ T W E & & \boxed{N} & T & Y \end{array}$$

Mnemonic tip Pronounce *seize* (16) as in English "**Says who?**"

Simple Arithmetical Expressions

deux <u>et</u> deux <u>font</u> quatre	$2 + 2 = 4$
trois <u>fois</u> cinq <u>font</u> quinze	$3 \times 5 = 15$
douze <u>moins</u> dix <u>font</u> deux	$12 - 10 = 2$
dix <u>divisés</u> <u>par</u> deux <u>font</u> cinq	$10 \div 2 = 5$

Fractions

½	*un demi*	a (one) half
⅓	*un tiers*	a (one) third
¼	*un quart*	a (one) fourth
⅕	*un cinquième*	a (one) fifth

Approximate Amounts

une dizaine	about ten
une quinzaine	about fifteen
une vingtaine	about twenty
une trentaine	about thirty
une quarantaine	about forty
une cinquantaine	about fifty
une soixantaine	about sixty
une centaine	about a hundred
un millier	about a thousand

Mnemonic tip	You can remember that *une quarantaine* is about 40 because there are 40 days in a "quarantine."

Ordinal Numbers: First to Twentieth

first	*premier, première*	1st	1er, 1re
second	*deuxième (second, seconde)*	2d	2^{e}
third	*troisième*	3d	3^{e}
fourth	*quatrième*	4th	4^{e}
fifth	*cinquième*	5th	5^{e}
sixth	*sixième*	6th	6^{e}

seventh	*septième*	7th	7ᵉ
eighth	*huitième*	8th	8ᵉ
ninth	*neuvième*	9th	9ᵉ
tenth	*dixième*	10th	10ᵉ
eleventh	*onzième*	11th	11ᵉ
twelfth	*douzième*	12th	12ᵉ
thirteenth	*treizième*	13th	13ᵉ
fourteenth	*quatorzième*	14th	14ᵉ
fifteenth	*quinzième*	15th	15ᵉ
sixteenth	*seizième*	16th	16ᵉ
seventeenth	*dix-septième*	17th	17ᵉ
eighteenth	*dix-huitième*	18th	18ᵉ
nineteenth	*dix-neuvième*	19th	19ᵉ
twentieth	*vingtième*	20th	20ᵉ

Some observations:

- You must learn the difference between cardinal and ordinal numbers. If you have trouble distinguishing between the two, just remember that we use cardinal numbers most of the time: *un, deux, trois* (one, two, three), and so on.

- Use ordinal numbers to express a certain order: *premier* (*première,* if the noun following is feminine), *deuxième, troisième* (first, second, third), and so on.

- *Premier* is the masculine singular form and *première* is the feminine singular form. Examples: *le premier homme* / the first man, *la première femme* / the first woman.

- The masculine singular form *second,* or the feminine singular form *seconde,* is used to mean "second" when there are only two. When there are more than two, *deuxième* is used: *le Second Empire,* because there were only two empires in France, but *la Deuxième République,* because there have been more than two republics in France.

- The raised letters in *1ᵉʳ* are the last two letters in the word *premier;* it is equivalent to our "st" in 1st. The raised letters in *1ʳᵉ* are the last two letters in the word *première,* which is the feminine singular form of "first."

The raised letter *e* after an ordinal number (for example, *2ᵉ*) stands for the *-ième* ending of a French ordinal number.

When referring to sovereigns or rulers, the only ordinal number used is *premier.* For all other designations, the cardinal numbers are used. The definite article "the" is used in English but not in French. Examples:

François 1ᵉʳ	*François Premier*	Francis the First
	BUT	
Louis XIV	*Louis Quatorze*	Louis the Fourteenth

§17.

Synonyms

Synonyms are words with the same or nearly the same meaning.

aide n.f., *secours* n.m.	aid, help
aimer mieux v., *préférer*	to like better, prefer
aliment n.m., *nourriture* n.f.	food, nourishment
anneau n.m., *bague* n.f.	ring (on finger)
arriver v., *se passer*	to happen, occur
aussitôt que conj., *dès que*	as soon as
auteur n.m., *écrivain* n.m.	author, writer
bâtiment n.m., *édifice,* n.m.	building, edifice
bâtir v., *construire*	to build, construct
beaucoup de adv., *bien des*	many
bref. brève adj., *court, courte*	brief, short
casser v., *rompre, briser*	to break
causer v., *parler*	to chat, talk
centre n.m., *milieu,* n.m.	center, middle
certain (certaine) adj., *sûr, sûre*	certain, sure
cesser v., *arrêter*	to cease, to stop
chagrin n.m., *souci* n.m.	sorrow, trouble, care, concern
chemin n.m., *route* n.f.	road, route
commencer à + infinitive, v., *se mettre à* + infinitive	to commence, begin, start
conseil n.m., *avis* n.m.	counsel, advice, opinion
content, (contente) adj., *heureux (heureuse)*	content, happy
de façon que conj., *de manière que*	so that, in such a way
décéder v., *mourir*	to die

adj.: adjective; adv.: adverb; conj.: conjunction; f.: feminine; m.: masculine; n.: noun; prep.: preposition; v.: verb

dégoût n.m., *répugnance* n.f.	disgust, repugnance
dérober v., *voler*	to rob, steal
désirer v., *vouloir*	to desire, want
disputer v., *contester*	to dispute, argue, contest
docteur n.m., *médecin,* n.m.	doctor, physician
embrasser v., *donner un baiser*	to embrace, hug; to give a kiss
employer v., *se servir de*	to employ, use, make use of
épouvanter v., *effrayer*	to frighten, terrify, scare
erreur n.f., *faute,* n.f.	error, fault, mistake
espèce n.f., *sorte,* n.f.	species, type, kind, sort
essayer de + infinitive, v., *tâcher de* + infinitive	to try, to attempt + infinitive
étrennes n.f., *cadeau* n.m.	Christmas gifts, present, gift
façon n.f., *manière,* n.f.	way, manner
fameux, (fameuse) adj., *célèbre*	famous, celebrated
fatigué, (fatiguée) adj., *épuisé, (épuisée)*	tired, fatigued, exhausted
favori, (favorite) adj., *préféré (préférée)*	favorite, preferred
fin n.f., *bout* n.m.	end
finir v., *terminer*	to finish, end, terminate
frémir v., *trembler*	to shiver, quiver, tremble
galette n.f., *gâteau* n.m.	cake
gaspiller v., *dissiper*	to waste, dissipate
gâter v., *abîmer*	to spoil, ruin, damage
glace n.f., *miroir* n.m.	hand mirror, mirror
grossier, grossière adj., *vulgaire*	gross, vulgar, cheap, common
habiter v., *demeurer*	to live (in), dwell, inhabit
haïr v., *détester*	to hate, detest
image n.f., *tableau* n.m.	image, picture
indiquer v., *montrer*	to indicate, show
jadis adv., *autrefois*	formerly, in times gone by

jeu n.m., *divertissement,* n.m.	game, amusement
labourer v, *travailler*	to labor, work
laisser v., *permettre*	to allow, permit
lier v., *attacher*	to tie, attach
lieu n.m., *endroit,* n.m.	place, spot, location
logis n.m. *habitation* n.f.	lodging, dwelling
lutter v., *combattre*	to struggle, fight, combat
maître n.m. *instituteur,* n.m.	master, teacher, instructor
maîtresse n.f. *institutrice,* n.f.	mistress, teacher, instructor
mauvais (mauvaise) adj., *méchant (méchante)*	bad, mean, nasty
mener v., *conduire*	to lead; to take (someone)
mince adj., *grêle*	thin, slender, skinny
naïf (naïve) adj., *ingénu (ingénue)*	naive, simple, innocent
net (nette) adj., *propre*	neat, clean
noces n.f., *mariage* n.m.	wedding, marriage
œuvre n.f., *travail* n.m.	work
ombre n.f., *obscurité* n.f.	shade, shadow, darkness
ombrelle n.f., *parasol* n.m.	sunshade, parasol, beach umbrella
parce que conj., *car*	because, for
pareil (pareille) adj., *égal (égale)*	similar, equivalent, equal
parvenir à v., *réussir à*	to succeed, to attain
pays n.m., *nation* n.f.	country, nation
pensée n.f., *idée,* n.f.	thought, idea
penser v., *réfléchir*	to think, reflect
penser à v., *songer à*	to think of; to dream of
professeur n.m., *maître,* n.m., *maîtresse,* n.f.	professor, teacher
puis adv., *ensuite*	then, afterwards
quand conj., *lorsque*	when
quelquefois adv., *parfois*	sometimes, at times
se rappeler v., *se souvenir de*	to recall, to remember

rester v., *demeurer*	to stay, to remain
sérieux (sérieuse) adj., *grave*	serious, grave
seulement adv., *ne* + verb + *que*	only
soin n.m., *attention* n.f.	care, attention
soulier n.m., *chaussure* n.f.	shoe, footwear
tout de suite adv., *immédiatement*	right away, immediately
triste adj., *malheureux (malheureuse)*	sad, unhappy
vêtements n.m., *habits,* n.m.	clothes, clothing
visage n.m., *figure* n.f.	face
vite adv., *rapidement*	quickly, rapidly

Mnemonic tip	*Bref* is brief and *court* is short because it contains the English word ''curt'' (brief, short).

Mnemonic tip	*Une chaussure* is a shoe because it contains *sur* / on, and you put it on your foot.

Mnemonic tip	*Une chaussette* is a sock because it's something like an anklet(te) sock.

Mnemonic tip	*Une parole* is a spoken word because when a prisoner is on ''*parole*'' he gives his word that he will behave in a civil manner.

Mnemonic tip	When you give someone *conseil,* you give him counsel, advice.

Mnemonic tip	When you *embrasser* a person, you put your *bras* / arms around that person.

§18.

Antonyms

Antonyms are words with opposite meanings.

absent (absente) adj, absent — *présent (présente)* adj., prese[nt]

acheter v., to buy — *vendre* v., to sell

agréable adj., pleasant, agreeable — *désagréable* adj., unpleasant, disagreeable

aimable adj., kind — *méchant (méchante)* adj., mean, nasty

aller v., to go — *venir* v., to come

ami (amie) n., friend — *ennemi (ennemie)* n., enemy

s'amuser refl. v., to enjoy oneself, to have a good time — *s'ennuyer* refl. v., to be bored

ancien (ancienne) adj., old, ancient — *nouveau (nouvel, nouvelle)* adj., new

avant prep., before — *après* prep., after

bas (basse) adj., low — *haut (haute)* adj., high

beau (bel, belle) adj., beautiful, handsome — *laid (laide)* adj., ugly

beaucoup (de) adv., much, many — *peu (de)* adv., little, some

beauté n.f., beauty — *laideur* n.f., ugliness

bête adj., stupid — *intelligent (intelligente)* adj., intelligent

bon (bonne) adj., good — *mauvais (mauvaise)* adj., bad

bonheur n.m., happiness — *malheur* n.m., unhappiness

chaud (chaude) adj., hot, warm — *froid (froide)* adj., cold

cher (chère) adj., expensive — *bon marché* cheap

content (contente) adj., glad, pleased — *mécontent (mécontente)* adj., displeased

adj.: adjective; adv.: adverb; conj.: conjunction; f.: feminine; m.: masculine; n.: noun; prep.: preposition; v.: verb

ourt (courte) adj., short	*long (longue)* adj., long
bout adv., standing	*assis (assise)* adj., seated, sitting
dans adv., inside	*dehors* adv., outside
mander v., to ask	*répondre* v., to reply
rnier (dernière) adj., last	*premier (première)* adj., first
rrière adv., prep., behind, in back of	*devant* adv., prep., in front of
ssous adv., prep., below, underneath	*dessus* adv., prep., above, over
fférent (différente) adj., different	*pareil (pareille)* adj., same, similar
ficile adj., difficult	*facile* adj., easy
mestique adj., domestic	*sauvage* adj., wild
nner v., to give	*recevoir* v., to receive
oite n.f., right	*gauche* n.f., left
nprunter v., to borrow	*prêter* v., to lend
trer (dans) v., to enter (in, into)	*sortir (de)* v., to go out (of, from)
t n.m., east	*ouest* n.m., west
roit (étroite) adj., narrow	*large* adj., wide
ble adj., weak	*fort (forte)* adj., strong
rmer v., to close	*ouvrir* v., to open
*n.f., end	*commencement* n.m., beginning
ir v., to finish	*commencer* v., to begin; *se mettre à* v., to begin + inf.
gner v., to win	*perdre* v., to lose
i (gaie) adj., gay, happy	*triste* adj., sad
and (grande) adj., large, tall, big	*petit (petite)* adj., small, little
os (grosse) adj., fat	*maigre* adj., thin
ossier (grossière) adj., coarse, impolite	*poli (polie)* adj., polite
ureux (heureuse) adj., happy	*malheureux (malheureuse)* adj., unhappy

ici adv., here
inutile adj., useless

là-bas adv., there
utile adj., useful

jamais adv., never
jeune adj., young
jeunesse n.f., youth
joli (jolie) adj., pretty
jour n.m., day

toujours adv., always
vieux (vieil, vieille) adj., old
vieillesse n.f., old age
laid (laide) adj., ugly
nuit n.f., night

léger (légère) adj., light
lentement adv., slowly

lourd (lourde) adj., heavy
vite adv., quickly

mal adv., badly
moderne adj., modern

bien adv., well
ancien (ancienne) adj.,
    ancient, old

moins adv., less
monter v., to go up
mourir v., to die
né (née) adj., past part., born

plus adv., more
descendre v., to go down
naître v., to be born
mort (morte) adj., past part.,
    died, dead

nord n.m., north
nouveau (nouvel, nouvelle)
    adj., new

sud n.m., south
vieux (vieil, vieille) adj., old

obéir (à) v., to obey
ôter v., to remove, to take off
oui adv., yes

désobéir (à) v., to disobey
mettre v., to put, to put on
non adv., no

paix n.f., peace
paraître v., to appear
paresseux (paresseuse) adj.,
    lazy
partir v., to leave
pauvre adj., poor
perdre v., to lose
plancher n.m., floor
plein (pleine) adj., full
poli (polie) adj., polite
possible adj., possible
prendre v., to take

guerre n.f., war
disparaître v., to disappear
travailleur (travailleuse) adj.,
    diligent
arriver v., to arrive
riche adj., rich
trouver v., to find
plafond n.m., ceiling
vide adj., empty
impoli (impolie) adj., impolite
impossible adj., impossible
donner v., to give

près (de) adv., prep., near

propre adj., clean

quelque chose pron., something

quelqu'un pron., someone, somebody

question n.f., question

refuser v., to refuse

réussir (à) v., to succeed (at, in)

rire v., to laugh

sans prep., without

silence n.m., silence

souvent adv., often

sur prep., on

sûr (sûre) adj., sure, certain

tôt adv., early

travailler v., to work

travailleur (travailleuse) adj., diligent, hardworking

vie n.f., life

vivre v., to live

vrai (vraie) adj., true

loin (de) adv., prep., far (from)

sale adj., dirty

rien pron., nothing

personne pron., nobody, no one

réponse n.f., answer, reply, response

accepter v., to accept

échouer (à) v., to fail (at, in)

pleurer v., to cry, to weep

avec prep., with

bruit n.m., noise

rarement adv., rarely

sous prep., under

incertain (incertaine) adj., unsure, uncertain

tard adv., late

jouer v., to play

paresseux (paresseuse) adj., lazy

mort n.f., death

mourir v., to die

faux (fausse) adj., false

| Mnemonic tip | The verb *mourir* (to die) has one *r* because a person dies once; *nourrir* (to nourish) has two *r*'s because a person is nourished more than once. |

| Mnemonic tip | The word *dessous* (below, underneath) contains *sous* (under). |

| Mnemonic tip | The word *dessus* (above, over) contains *sus,* which reminds you of *sur* (on). |

| Mnemonic tip | *Perdre* means "to lose" because perdition is a place for lost souls. |

| Mnemonic tip | Detroit, a city in Michigan, is on the Detroit River, which is narrow *(étroit)* in spots. |

| Mnemonic tip | A floor *(le plancher)* was originally made of wooden planks. |

| Mnemonic tip | Pronounce *bonne* as in the English word "bun." |

| Mnemonic tip | You "mount" a mountain when you *monte une montagne.* |

| Mnemonic tip | You go **a**way when you *p**a**rtir* and you go **o**ut when you *s**o**rtir. P**a**rtir* and "**a**way" contain **a**'s. *S**o**rtir* and "g**o o**ut" contain **o**'s. |

| Mnemonic tip | If you don't know your right from your left, *droite* contains "it" and so does "right." |

§19.

Cognates

In addition to studying synonyms in §17. and antonyms in §18., another good way to increase your vocabulary is to become aware of cognates. A *cognate* is a word whose origin is the same as another word in another language. There are many cognates in French and English whose spelling is sometimes identical or very similar. Most of the time, the meaning is the same or similar; sometimes they appear to be related because of similar spelling, but they are not true cognates. You will find a list of these "false cognates" or "tricky words" in §20.

Generally speaking, certain endings, or suffixes, of French words have English equivalents.

EXAMPLES

French Suffix	Equivalent English Suffix	French Word	English Word
-able	-able	*adorable*	adorable
		aimable	amiable (likeable)
-aire	-ary	*le dictionnaire*	dictionary
-eux	-ous	*fameux*	famous
-euse		*fameuse*	
-ieux	-ous	*gracieux*	gracious
-ieuse		*gracieuse*	
-iste	-ist	*le (la) dentiste*	dentist
-ité	-ity	*la qualité*	quality
-ment	-ly	*correctement*	correctly
-mettre	-mit	*admettre*	admit
-oire	-ory	*la mémoire*	memory
-phie	-phy	*la photographie*	photography
-scrire	-scribe	*transcrire*	transcribe

A French word that contains the circumflex accent (^) over a vowel means that there used to be an *s* right after that vowel.

EXAMPLES

hâte / haste	*hôtel* / hostel
pâte / paste	*honnête* / honest
bâtard / bastard	*plâtre* / plaster
bête / beast	*île* / isle
fête / feast	*vêpres* / vespers
mât / mast	*prêtre* / priest

But you don't always get a cognate if you insert an *s* right after the vowel that contains a circumflex.

EXAMPLES

gâteau / cake	*bêler* / to bleat
bâtiment / building	*âme* / soul

Mnemonic tip	If you confuse *le gâteau* (cake) with *le bateau* (boat) because you can't remember which one contains the circumflex accent, remember that the ^ in *gâteau* is the icing on top of the cake!

ricky Words

"alse friends" are look-alikes but have different meanings.

ualités n.f., pl. news
  eports
uel adj. present, present-
  lay
uellement adv. at present
dition n.f. bill (check)
endre v. to wait

le adj., fem. beautiful
ir v. to bless
sser v. to wound
s n.m. arm
  n.m. goal

inet n.m. office; study
  conj. because
ser v. to chat; to cause
e n.f. cellar, basement
ir n.f. flesh
t n.m. cat
se n.f. thing
n n.m. corner
mment adv. how
férence n.f. lecture
ne n.m. skull
yon n.m. pencil
t n.f. tooth
e v. to say, to tell
  n.f. dowry

teur n.m. publisher
ence n.f. gasoline

fin n.f. end
flèche n.f. arrow
fort adj., n. strong
four n.m. oven
front n.m. forehead

grand adj., m. tall, big, large
grave adj. serious

haïr v. to hate

journal n.m. newspaper

large adj. wide, broad
lecture n.f. reading
librairie n.f. bookstore

magasin n.m. store
main n.f. hand
marine n.f. navy; seascape
médecin n.m. doctor,
  physician
médecine n.f. medicine
  (study of)
médicament n.m. medicine
mine n.f. facial appearance
monnaie n.f. change (coins)

on pers. pron. one, someone, they
ours n.m. bear (animal)

pain n.m. bread
pal n.m. pale, stake (for
  punishment)

par prep. by
personnel adj. personal
pie n.f. magpie (bird)
pile n.f. battery; pile, heap
place n.f. plaza, place
plate adj., fem. flat
pour prep. for
prune n.f. plum
pruneau n.m. prune

raisin n.m. grape
raisin sec n.m. raisin
râpe n.f. grater (cheese)
rose adj. pink

rose n. rose
rue n.f. street
sable n.m. sand
sale adj. dirty, soiled
sensible adj. sensitive
son n.m. sound
stage n.m. training course of
  study
stylo n.m. pen

tôt adv. early
user v. to wear out
vent n.m. wind (air)
vie n.f. life

French-English Vocabulary

...rep. at, to

...oins que *conj.* unless

...if, active *adj.* active

...oport *n.m.* airport

...eusement *adv.* frightfully

... *form of* **avoir**

...able *adj.* amiable, likeable, pleasant, kind

...er *v.* to love; **aimer bien** to like

...magne *n.f.* Germany

...mand *n.m.* German (language); **Allemand, Allemande** *n.* German (person)

...r *v.* to go; **s'en aller** to go away

...z-vous-en! go away!

...ns! let's go!

...èrement *adv.* bitterly

...i, amie *n.* friend

...our *n.m.* love

...usant, amusante *adj.* funny, amusing

... *n.m.* year

...cien, ancienne *adj.* old, ancient

...glais *n.m.* English (language); **Anglais, Anglaise** *n.* English (person)

...gleterre *n.f.* England

...eler *v.* to call; **s'appeler** *reflexive v.* to call oneself, to be named

...ès *prep., adv.* after; **après-midi** afternoon

...re *n.m.* tree

...ent *n.m.* money

...e *n.f.* Asia

...eoir *v.* to seat; **s'asseoir** *reflexive v.* to sit down; **asseyez-vous!** sit down!

...ez (de) *adv.* enough (of); **assez bien** quite well, well enough

...ieds-toi! sit down!

... to the, at the; contraction of **à + le**

...ourd'hui *adv.* today

---

adjective; adv.: adverb; conj.: conjunction; f.: feminine; m.: masculine; n.: noun; ...lural; prep.: preposition; pron.: pronoun; sing.: singular; v.: verb

aussi *adv.* also, too
aussi . . . que *conj.* as . . . as
Australie *n.f.* Australia
auteur *n.m.* author; **une femme auteur** woman author
autre *adj.* other; *pron.* another
autrefois *adv.* formerly
aux to the, at the; contraction of **à + les**
avec *prep.* with
avez *v. form of* **avoir**
avocat *n.m.* lawyer; **une avocate** woman lawyer
avoir *v.* to have

bas *n.m.* stocking; *adv.* low; **en bas** down, downstairs; *adj.* **bas, basse** low
beau *adj. m.* handsome, beautiful
beaucoup (de) *adv.* many, much (of)
bel *adj. m.* handsome, beautiful
belle *adj. f.* beautiful, handsome
bénir *v.* to bless
besoin *n.m.* need; **avoir besoin de** to need, to have need of
bibliothèque *n.f.* library
bien *adv.* well
bientôt *adv.* soon
billet *n.m.* ticket, note
blanc, blanche *adj.* white
blesser *v.* to injure, to wound
boire *v.* to drink
bon, bonne *adj.* good
bonbons *n.m.* candies
bouche *n.f.* mouth (of a person); **la gueule** (mouth of an animal)
but *n.m* goal

ça *pron.* shortening of **cela**
cadeau *n.m.* gift, present
café *n.m.* coffee
cahier *n.m.* notebook
campagne *n.f.* country(side)
catholique *n.m.f.* Catholic
ce *demons. adj.* this; **ce stylo** this pen; **ce livre** this book; **ce garçon** this boy

cela *pron.* that; **Aimez-vous cela?** Do you
 like that?
chanter *v.* to sing
chanteur, chanteuse *n.m.f.* singer
chapeau *n.m.* hat
chaque *adj.* each
chaud, chaude *adj.* warm, hot
chaussette *n.f.* sock
chaussure *n.f.* shoe
chef *n.m.* chief, boss, chef
cheveu, cheveux *n.m.* hair
chez *prep.* at the place of, at the home of,
 at the shop of; **chez moi** at my place
choisir *v.* to choose, to select
chose *n.f.* thing; **quelque chose** something
cinéma *n.m.* movies (theater)
clé, clef *n.f.* key
coin *n.m.* corner
combien (de) *adv.* how much (of), how
 many (of)
comprendre *v.* to understand
copain *n.m.,* **copine** *n.f.* pal, buddy
cravate *n.f.* necktie
crayon *n.m.* pencil
croire *v.* to believe
cruel, cruelle *adj.* cruel

dame *n.f.* lady
dans *prep.* in
de *prep.* of, from
dehors *adv.* outside
déjà *adv.* already; **déjà vu** already seen
dent *n.f.* tooth
depuis *adv.* since; **depuis longtemps** for a
 long time
dernier, dernière *adj.* last
des of the, from the; contraction of **de** +
 les; some
dimanche *n.m.* Sunday
dire *v.* to say, to tell; **vouloir dire** to mean
donc *conj.* therefore, consequently
donner *v.* to give
dont *pron.* of which, whose
dormir *v.* to sleep

douche *n.f.* shower (bath)

douter *v.* to doubt

drôle *adj.* funny, droll

du of the, from the; contraction of **de + le**; some

dû *past participle of* **devoir**; ought to, must

eau *n.f.* water

école *n.f.* school; **à l'école** in (at, to) school

écouter *v.* to listen (to)

écrire *v.* to write

écrivons *v. form of* **écrire**

égal, égaux, égale, égales *adj.* equal

église *n.f.* church

en *pron.* of it, of them, some of it, some of them; *prep.* in

encore *adv.* still, yet, again

encre *n.f.* ink

enregistrer *v.* to record (on a tape, record)

enseigner *v.* to teach

entendre *v.* to hear, to understand

enthousiasme *n.m.* enthusiasm

entre *prep.* between; *also a v. form of* **entrer (dans)** to enter (into)

envers *prep.* toward

environ *adv.* nearly, about

envoyer *v.* to send; **envoyer chercher** to send for

Espagne *n.f.* Spain

espagnol *n.m.* Spanish (language); **Espagnol, Espagnole** *n.* Spanish (person)

est *present indicative of* **être**

Etats-Unis *n.m.pl.* United States

été *n.m.* summer; also *past participle of* **être**

être *v.* to be

étudiant, étudiante *n.m.* student

étudier *v.* to study

eu *past participle of* **avoir**

faim *n.f.* hunger; **avoir faim** to be hungry

faire *v.* to do, to make; **faire un voyage** to take a trip

falloir *v.* to be necessary; **il faut** it is necessary

faux, fausse *adj.* false

favori, favorite *adj.* favorite

femme *n.f.* woman; when possessive, wife; **ma femme** my wife

fête *n.f.* feast, holiday, party

feu *n.m.* fire; **le feu rouge** red light (traffic)

février *n.m.* February

fille *n.f.* daughter; **la jeune fille** girl; **une école de filles** girls' school

fils *n.m.* son

finir *v.* to finish, to end

forêt *n.f.* forest

fourchette *n.f.* fork

français *n.m.* French (language); **Français, Française** *n.* French (person)

franchement *adv.* frankly

frère *n.m.* brother

fromage *n.m.* cheese

fuir *v.* to flee, to run away; *past participle* **fui**

garçon *n.m.* boy

gâteau *n.m.* cake

gentil, gentille *adj.* nice, pleasant

gentiment *adv.* gently

gomme *n.f.* eraser (rubber)

grand, grande *adj.* great, big, large; **un grand magasin** department store

Grande Bretagne *n.f.* Great Britain

gris, grise *adj.* gray

gros, grosse *adj.* big, fat, large

heureusement *adv.* fortunately, happily

heureux, heureuse *adj.* happy

homme *n.m.* man

honneur *n.m.* honor

huître *n.f.* oyster

ici *adv.* here

île *n.f.* isle, island

immeuble *n.m.* apartment building

interrompre *v.* to interrupt
italien *n.m.* Italian (language); **Italien, Italienne** *n.* Italian (person)

janvier *n.m.* January
jeune *adj.* young
jeune fille *n.f.* girl
joli, jolie *adj.* pretty
jouer *v.* to play
jouet *n.m.* toy
jour *n.m.* day
journal *n.m.* newspaper
journée *n.f.* (all) day (long)

la *definite article, f.* the; *also direct object pronoun, f. sing.* it, her
laid, laide *adj.* ugly
laideur *n.f.* ugliness
laver *v.* to wash (something or someone); **se laver** *reflex. verb* to wash oneself
le *definite article, m.* the; *also direct object pronoun, m. sing.* it, him
lent, lente *adj.* slow
lentement *adv.* slowly
les *definite article, m. and f.* the; *also direct object pronoun, m. and f., pl.* them (people or things)
leur *possessive adj.* their; *also indirect object pron.* to them
lire *v.* to read; *past participle* **lu**
lit *n.m.* bed; *also present indicative, 3d person sing. of* **lire**
livre *n.m.* book; **la livre** pound
Londres *n.m.* London
long, longue *adj.* long
longtemps *adv.* long time; **depuis longtemps** since a long time, for a long time
lorsque *adv.* when; *synonym of* **quand**
lui *indirect object pron., 3d person sing.* to him, to her
lundi *n.m.* Monday

ma *possessive adj., f. sing.* my; **ma maison** my house
magasin *n.m.* store; **un grand magasin** department store
magazine *n.m.* magazine
maintenant *adv.* now
mais *conj.* but
maison *n.f.* house
malheur *n.m.* unhappiness
malheureusement *n.f.* unfortunately
manger *v.* to eat
marcher *v.* to walk, to march, to run (a machine)
mardi *n.m.* Tuesday
mars *n.m.* March
matin *n.m.* morning; **le matin** in the morning
médecin *n.m.* doctor
médecine *n.f.* medicine (profession)
médicament *n.m.* medicine (that you take)
meilleur, meilleure *adj.* better
mer *n.f.* sea
mère *n.f.* mother
mettre *v.* to put, to place; to put on (clothing)
mieux *adv.* better
monnaie *n.f.* change (money); coins
monsieur *n.m.* gentleman, sir, Mr.
mourir *v.* to die

naître *v.* to be born; *past participle* **né**
natation *n.f.* swimming
noir, noire *adj.* black
nom *n.m.* name
nouveau, nouvel, nouvelle *adj.* new

œil *n.m.* eye; **les yeux** eyes
œuf *n.m.* egg
oiseau *n.m.* bird
on *personal pron., 3d person sing.* one (they)
oser *v.* to dare
ou *conj.* or; **où** *adv.* where
ouvrir *v.* to open; *past participle* **ouvert**

pain *n.m.* bread

papier *n.m.* paper

par *prep.* by; **par terre** on the floor, on the ground

parapluie *n.m.* umbrella

parc *n.m.* park

paresse *n.f.* laziness

paresseux, paresseuse *adj.* lazy

parler *v.* to talk, to speak

partir *v.* to leave; *past participle* **parti**

passer *v.* to spend (time); to go by, to pass by, to pass

pendant *prep.* during; **pendant que** *conj.* while

perdre *v.* to lose; *past participle* **perdu(e)(s)**

père *n.m.* father

perspicacité *n.f.* perspicacity, insight

peu (de) *adv.* little (of)

peur *n.f.* fear; **avoir peur** to be afraid, to feel afraid

peut *present indicative of* **pouvoir**

pied *n.m.* foot; **aller à pied** to walk

plage *n.f.* beach, seashore

pleuvoir *v.* to rain; *past participle* **plu**

plus *adv.* more; **plus de, plus que** more than

plusieurs *adv.* several

poule *n.f.* hen

poupée *n.f.* doll

pousser *v.* to push, to bud (flowers)

pouvoir *v.* to be able, can

précise *adj.* precise, precisely

prendre *v.* to take

presse *n.f.* press (printing)

public, publique *adj.* public

puis *adv.* then

quand *adv.* when; *synonym of* **lorsque**

quel, quelle, quels, quelles *adj.* which, what

quelque(s) *adj.* some; **quelque chose** something

quelquefois *adv.* sometimes

qui *pron.* who, whom

qui est-ce qui *pron.* who
quitter *v.* to leave (a person or place)
quoi *pron.* what (as obj. of a prep.); **avec quoi** with what

rang *n.m.* rank, row
restaurant *n.m.* restaurant
rire *v.* to laugh; laughter
robe *n.f.* dress
rose *n.f.* rose; *adj.* pink
rue *n.f.* street

samedi *n.m.* Saturday
sans *prep.* without
se *reflexive pron.* himself, herself, oneself
sec, sèche *adj.* dry
seize sixteen
semaine *n.f.* week
si *conj.* if
sœur *n.f.* sister
soir *n.m.* evening; **le soir** in the evening
son *n.m.* sound; *possessive adj.* his, her, its
sont *v. form of* être
sous *prep.* under
souvent *adv.* often
stylo *n.m.* pen
sucette *n.f.* lollipop; **sucer** *v.* to suck
sur *prep.* on

tenir *v.* to hold
thé *n.m.* tea
très *adv.* very
trop (de) *adv.* too much (of), too many (of)
trouver *v.* to find; **se trouver** *reflexive v.* to be located
tuer *v.* to kill

un *indefinite article, m. sing.* a, an (one); *fem.,* **une**

vacances *n.f.pl.* vacation; **les grandes vacances** summer vacation

vache *n.f.* cow

vais *present indicative of* **aller**

vendre *v.* to sell

venir *v.* to come

vent *n.m.* wind; **il fait du vent** it's windy

viande *n.f.* meat

vient *present indicative of* **venir**

vieux, vieil, vieille *adj.* old

vin *n.m.* wine

vingt twenty

voir *v.* to see; *past participle* **vu**

voyage *n.m.* trip; **faire un voyage** to take a trip, go on a trip; **Bon voyage!** Have a good trip!

y *adverbial pron.* there, in it, on it

yeux *n.m.* eyes; **l'œil** the eye

zèbre *n.m.* zebra

Index

References are to § numbers in this book.

191